TWAYNE'S WORLD AUTHORS SERIES
A Survey of the World's Literature

SPAIN

Janet W. Díaz, University of North Carolina, Chapel Hill
EDITOR

Luis Cernuda

TWAS 455

Luis Cernuda

LUIS CERNUDA

By SALVADOR JIMENEZ-FAJARDO

New England College

TWAYNE PUBLISHERS
A DIVISION OF G. K. HALL & CO., BOSTON

Library of Congress Cataloging in Publication Data

Jiménez-Fajardo, Salvador.
  Luis Cernuda.

  (Twayne's world authors series ; TWAS 455 : Spain)
  Bibliography: p. 165-67
  Includes index.
  1. Cernuda, Luis—Criticism and interpretation.
I. Title.
PQ6605.E7Z7   861'.6'2   77-27247
ISBN 0-8057-6292-2

MANUFACTURED IN THE UNITED STATES OF AMERICA

To My Parents

En tu tierra y afuera de tu tierra
Siempre traían fielmente
El encanto de España, en ellos no perdido.

Luis Cernuda, Díptico Español, II

Contents

About the Author

Salvador Jiménez-Fajardo was born in Spain and lived in France and Canada before coming to the United States. He has an M.A. in English literature from the University of Montreal and was the recipient of a Special Woodrow Wilson Fellowship. He obtained his Ph.D. in Romance Languages from the University of Chicago. He is currently teaching literature and language at New England College, a liberal arts institution in New Hampshire. Mr. Jiménez-Fajardo is the author of *Claude Simon,* a recent volume on the French novelist in the Twayne World Author Series, and has published on contemporary French and Spanish literature.

search for idealized reality; likewise his antipathy to Christian eschatology arises from the concept of time it embodies, the forward march of history from creation to judgment. From the application of his personal ideology and aesthetic credo to his own circumstance emerges the individual myth to whose elaboration contribute all the facets and moments of his life.

An ideal whose attainment approaches the mystical is only infrequently susceptible of realization. In its shadow daily living, when it refuses the structuration toward myth, appears a paltry jumble of meaningless deeds. The world of present man, social convention, will seem doubly oppressive to Cernuda, because of his poetic aspirations as well as his homosexual preference; so that one of his most natural reactions to this human environment is rejection. Thus, as landmarks along his creative journey will recur moments of refusal, of retreat, or, more rarely, instances of transcendent calm, all aspects of his unabating involvement with the real. And it is because these dispositions do persist with varying intensity throughout the poet's career and are integrated by his poetic language that the straightforward organization of this study along the biographical axis imposed itself. For the unity that makes of Cernuda's twelve books of poetry a self-consistent collection is the constancy of his struggle with matter and time; and the thrust of his work's evolution is a likewise singleminded attention to the quality of his art.

The first chapter of this essay is mainly a biographical sketch of Luis Cernuda in which I have attempted to situate him in the literary climate of his early years and trace his development thereafter. I refer with frequency to his own evaluation of the facts insofar as they involved actual events or personal reactions to them. I consider that Cernuda's formative period with respect to his poetry extends to the publication of *Invocaciones (Invocations)* and have therefore devoted the second chapter to his work up to and including this collection. The two subsequent books of poems that he published show a poet in full possession of his art and under the sway of powerful internal forces calling for expression. They contain some of his greatest and most extensive compositions. In consequence of this, Chapters 3 and 4 of this study are longer and also somewhat more involved. The pattern of one chapter per book of poems is followed in Chapters 5 through 7. Also, it is Cernuda's poetic output that has mainly drawn my attention; I have dwelt lightly on his critical work, except when it applied to his own verse, as well as the short stories of *Variaciones sobre tema mexicano. (Variations on a Mexican Theme)*. Although deserving of closer examination, I felt that these prose writings did not belong within the compass of the present study.

While the nature of this book did not allow for the sustained exegesis that Cernuda's poetry calls for, it is hoped that the details provided may hint at the multilayered depth underlying its evocative beauty. All translations, except where noted, are my own. In them I have tried to remain as true to the original as English syntax permitted, preferring accuracy at all times.

I wish to thank my wife, Lisa Koch Fajardo, for her boundless patience and diligent application in typing my manuscript through its various stages of growth as well as for her ever perceptive suggestions. This book could not have been written without her. I am grateful to Dean Erwin Jaffe and New England College for the material assistance they graciously extended to me. I also want to thank the Fondo de Cultura Económica of Mexico for allowing me to quote and translate from their edition of *La realidad y el deseo* as well as New York University Press for permission to cite from the anthology *The Poetry of Luis Cernuda*, edited by Derek Harris and Anthony Edkins.

SALVADOR JIMÉNEZ-FAJARDO

New England College

Chronology

1952	Moves to Mexico.
1956	Completes *Con las horas contadas*.
1960–1962	Visiting Professor at UCLA and San Francisco State College.
1958	Third edition of *La realidad y el deseo*.
1962	Completes *Desolación de la quimera*.
1963	November, death of Cernuda.
1964	Fourth edition of *La realidad y el deseo*.

CHAPTER 1

The Poet and His Time

I *The Generation of 1925*

FOR Cernuda the principal trait of the generation of poets of 1925—or 1927—is a predilection for metaphors: "The first characteristic of the group, although not born with it and existing previously . . . is the special cultivation of metaphor, a poetic cultivation that the group gathers and appropriates."[1] Here he finds no difference between this inclination in Spain and those of other literary movements of the period, all displaying a marked reaction against the aestheticist tendencies of the late nineteenth century. It was an antipathy to the tenets of modernism that led these Spanish poets away, in particular, from the idea that certain words or subjects are intrinsically poetic and toward an emphasis on the interpretation of reality through imagery.

This conception of poetics was not new. The romantics themselves had long before emphasized it, and Shelley's enthusiastic assertion that poetry "creates anew the universe" could be endorsed by any member of the generation of 1925, certainly by Cernuda himself. Of course, these young poets had remained sympathetic to the romantic and later to the symbolist tradition of Rimbaud's *poète voyant*. But craftsmanship was at least of equal importance to them, and in this respect it is to the Spanish classics that they turned, to the Golden Age and even earlier. There was a renewed interest in traditional meters and stanzas. Cernuda's first book of poems, *Perfil del aire, (The Air's Profile)* contains thirteen *décimas* (a verse form of Spanish origin of ten octosyllabic lines), and sixteen other compositions in assonant quatrains. Lorca composed a *Soledad* in honor of Fray Luis de León in the *lira*[2] form, while Gerardo Diego wrote an article entitled "The Return to the Strophe" in *Carmen*,[3] a magazine publishing the group's poetry, in which he announced: "We make *décimas*, we make sonnets, we make *liras* because we want to."[4]

The enthusiasm for classicism culminated in 1927 with a homage to Góngora, commemorating the tercentenary of his death. The young poets found in their great predecessor the concentrated metaphorical language and attention to craftsmanship that characterized their own aims. Also, the effort of comprehension required of Góngora's reader could not but please them; some saw in it an early form of Mallarmé's calculated obscurity, which would set apart the worthy reader of poetry from a broader public. It was the participation of all the principal poets of the group in this commemoration that led later critics to call it the Generation of 1927. Cernuda, although he admits the importance of that event and includes Góngora's influence as one of the possible coalescing forces in their inspiration, finds it an unsatisfactory criterion of nomenclature. He himself claims more important influences among the classics such as Garcilaso, princi- pally, and also Aldana, among others. Nor does he accept the label "generation of the dictatorship", finding the linking of the poets to the *directorado* of Primo de Rivera demeaning. His decision to use 1925 as a more adequate date of recognition stems from its being "a middle term in the appearance of their first books":[5] F. García Lorca's *Libro de poemas* (1921); Gerardo Diego's *Imagen* (1922); Pedro Salinas' *Pre- sagios* (1923); Emilio Prados' *Tiempo* (1925); Rafael Alberti's *Marinero en tierra* (1925); Manuel Altolaguirre's *Las islas invitadas* (1926); Cer- nuda's *Perfil del aire* (1927); Jorge Guillén's *Cántico* (1926); and Vicente Aleixandre's *Ámbito* (1928).

Another danger in choosing 1927 as the central date for this poetic generation lies in the overemphasis which Góngora's tercentenary would lay on the formal or "pure" aspects of their poetry. In his essay on the group Cernuda underlines precisely the fact that this is but one tendency and by no means a sustained one. Of equal, if not greater, importance would be for him their openness to foreign influences, that of surrealism in particular. As one of those who were most visibly affected by the French movement and who went beyond it, he was able to discern quite clearly its impact on his generation. He warns: "It would be a grave error to see it as merely another literary movement among those that had previously appeared, because of all of them, surrealism was the only one which had both an historical reason for existing and intellectual content."[6] As a generalized pro- test against basic supports of society such as religion, politics, and morality, surrealism found fertile ground in the decaying ambiance of

Spain's 1920s. Surrealist texts were translated in such magazines as
Alfar and *Litoral*; already in 1922 Breton had given a lecture in the
Ateneo of Barcelona, and Aragon lectured in the Residencia de
estudiantes of Madrid on April 18, 1925. In this respect also Cernuda
stood slightly apart from the other members of his generation. His
understanding of surrealism and of other alien poetic movements past
and present was probably more solid—he traveled to France, as we
shall see, and read the original works—and he was more attuned to
foreign ideas. But the strength of Cernuda's poetry, seen among that
of his peers, is highly individual. The presence of a great poet was felt
immediately by those who cared to read with attention, and it was not
hyperbole for Lorca to propose a jubilant salute honoring his fellow
Andalusian, "great poet of the mystery, most delicate poet Luis
Cernuda, for whom must be made over, since the seventeenth
century, the word divine, and to whom must be extended again
water, reed, and penumbra for his incredible renovated swan."[7]

II *Cernuda*

Lorca's speech, delivered at a banquet in Cernuda's honor on April
20, 1936, was occasioned by the publication of his collected verse
under the title *La realidad y el deseo (Reality and Desire)* on April 1 of
the same year. Cernuda had failed to have much of his work published following the appearance in 1927 of his first collection of
poetry, *Perfil del aire.*[8] With the exception of *Donde habite el olvido
(Where Oblivion Dwells)*[9] issued by *Signo* in 1934, four other books of
poems had remained unprinted. Such difficulties of publication,
coupled with the mixed reviews that greeted the appearance of *Perfil
del aire,* confirmed still further the poet's already marked reticence.
He was affected most deeply by what was in his estimation the unjust
criticism of his first volume. For although he completed a degree in
law in 1925, he had soon realized that poetry was his true calling and
felt all the more keenly any unfair evaluation of his work.

Luis Cernuda y Bidón was born in Seville September 21, 1902, the
youngest of three children—he had two older sisters—fathered by
a colonel in a regiment of engineers.[10] He obtained his *bachillerato*
(the equivalent of a high school degree) at the school of the *padres
escolapios* (Piarist Fathers) and enrolled at the University of Seville in
1919 to study law. His father died in 1920 and his family took up
residence at the calle del Aire, a quiet street where he composed his
first poems and where he remained until the death of his mother in
1928. In *Ocnos*, his book of prose poems, he describes himself in

those years as a sensitive and introspective youth, loving solitude and
highly responsive to the less apparent beauties of his surroundings:
"with the vision of that hidden beauty there slipped slowly into his
soul, nailing itself into it, a feeling of solitude unknown to him until
then."[11] He took classes in Spanish literature with Salinas as his
teacher at the University of Seville, but his timidity was such that the
latter was totally unaware of his existence and realized later in profound surprise that in his classes had sat "the finest, most delicate,
most elegant poet born to Seville since Bécquer."[12] In Cernuda's last
year at the university (1924–1925), he and Salinas became better acquainted. The older poet—only thirty-two himself—encouraged
Cernuda in his creative efforts, his reading of the classics, and
recommended that he learn French in order to become familiar with
French poetry. Also through Salinas Cernuda met Juan Ramón
Jiménez in September, 1925. It was probably owing to the help of
these two friends that nine of Cernuda's early poems appeared in the
Revista de Occidente in December, 1925. Subsequently, other
magazines such as *Litoral, La verdad,* and *Verso y prosa* were to
publish his work.

In the hope of entering a diplomatic career, Cernuda visited
Madrid in 1927. There he was introduced to Ortega y Gasset,
Eugenio d'Ors, Guillermo de Torre, Valle-Inclán, and other major
writers. That same year saw the appearance of *Perfil del aire* as a
supplement to the magazine *Litoral* edited by Emilio Prados and
Manuel Altolaguirre. Cernuda awaited this event with anguished
impatience and upon the volume's appearance he recalls: "The copies
were next to my bed during the night. I believe I hardly slept and
those poets who remember the appearance of their first book will
understand my lack of sleep."[13] As we mentioned above, the reviews
were mixed. The poet was particularly sensitive to repeated assertions of Guillén's influence on his verse and took pains thenceforward
to dispel such impressions. The core of his argument was that
Cántico, the first volume of Guillén's poetry, did not appear until
1928, and that any similarities of inspiration should be attributed to
both poets' reading of Mallarmé, directly in the case of Cernuda,
indirectly and through Valéry in that of Guillén.[14] Cernuda never
forgot this rebuff by the critics, and it remained more prominent in
his mind than other highly favorable comments the volume also
elicited from, among others, José Bergamín, who underlined the
basic differences between Cernuda and Guillén, and the Catalan

Lluis Montanyá, who praised the craftsmanship and purity of the poems.

Since another aspect of his early poetry which seemed to displease reviewers was its adherence to classical forms, Cernuda, following the maxim "That which they censure in you, cultivate it, for that is you," (PL, 183) wrote *Egloga, elegía, oda (Eclogue, Elegy, Ode).*[15] The book contains the poems indicated in its title as well as the shorter "Homenaje" ("Homage") originally published in the magazine *Carmen* as "Homenaje a Fray Luis de León." All four poems exhibit great facility with classical meter. This display of virtuosity did not satisfy Cernuda, however, although it demonstrated his solid "craftsmanship". Soon he would move away from the more obvious strictures of literary tradition and into the experiment with surrealism.

At the bookstore of Sánchez Cuesta in Madrid, where he worked for a time, Cernuda had been reading Aragon, Eluard, Breton, and other surrealist writers. He saw his own impatience echoed in these books: "Surrealism, with its aims and technique, had won my sympathy. Reading those first books by Aragon, by Breton, by Eluard, by Crevel, I realized how the uneasiness and daring that found voice in these same books was also mine. A young man alone, with none of the supports that, thanks to fortune and connections, society grants to so many, I could not but feel hostility toward that society in the midst of which I lived as a stranger. There existed in me another reason for discordance, even deeper, but I prefer not to enter into that now" (PL, 184). The other reason for his dissatisfaction was the social stigma attached to his homosexuality. Surrealism would also allow him to express this preference freely and help him to come to terms with its consequences.

In the fall of 1928, Salinas found a position for Cernuda as reader in Spanish at the University of Toulouse, solving temporarily his economic problems—his inheritance had been small—and providing him with the opportunity to go to the country of origin of surrealism. He traveled to Paris during vacation, gaining respite from the drabness of Toulouse itself. He wrote his first surrealist poems upon his return to Toulouse and the remainder of *Un río, un amor (A River, A Love)*, his third book, back in Madrid after the spring term. The last years of the Primo de Rivera dictatorship, with the political and social disintegration that accompanied them, made the rebellious tenets of surrealism all the more attractive to him. He completed his next book, *Los placeres prohibidos (Forbidden Pleasures)*, in 1932 and with it left behind surrealism as a literary technique; he never had wholly adhered to the more extreme aspects of the movement, such as automatic writing. *Donde habite el olvido (Where Oblivion Dwells)* was begun the same year under the influence of his reading of Bécquer and the repercussions of an unhappy love affair. In 1933 a selection of Cernuda's poetry was published by Altolaguirre in his series "La tentativa poética." It was entitled *La invitación a la poesía (Invitation to Poetry)* and contained nineteen poems taken from *Perfil del aire* and other unpublished material. That same year Cernuda wrote an endorsement of the ideas of *Octubre*, a revolutionary review published by Alberti, in which he expressed his solidarity with the Communist cause. He also contributed to it the poem "Vientres sentados" ("Seated Bellies") from *Forbidden Pleasures*. In 1931, Spain had become a republic. Although political corruption still existed and factionalism weakened the effectiveness of the government, there seemed to be greater hope for renewal. It was this situation which permitted, for instance, the publication of a magazine such as *Octubre*. In 1934 Cernuda was traveling with the *Misiones pedagógicas* [16] and contributing articles to the *Heraldo de Madrid*. *Where Oblivion Dwells* came out this same year, and in 1935 he started the poems that were to become *Invocaciones a las gracias del mundo (Invocations to the World's Graces)*, a title later shortened to *Invocations*. At this time he began to study Hölderlin and translated some of his poems with the help of the German poet Hans Gebser. The translations appeared in 1936 in *Cruz y raya*. The same house published the first edition of *La realidad y el deseo (Reality and Desire)*, also in 1936. In July, 1936, although the Civil War had broken out in Spain, Cernuda managed to leave the country as secretary to the republican ambassador to France, Alvaro de Albornoz. He returned from Paris in September and wrote numerous articles for a variety of newspapers in Madrid. In 1938, with the help of Stanley Richardson, an English poet, he obtained a post at the Cranleigh School in Surrey as assistant to the Spanish teacher. In January, 1939, he became lecturer at the University of Glasgow, where he completed *Las nubes (The Clouds)* in 1940. He had also begun to write *Ocnos*, a book of prose poems mainly on the theme of his Andalusian childhood. In 1940, the second edition of *Reality and Desire* appeared in Mexico under the auspices of José Bergamín; it contained seven collections of poems including *The Clouds*. From 1943 to 1945 he taught at Cambridge while at work on *Vivir sin estar viviendo (Living Without Being Alive)*. After two years at the Spanish Institute in London, where he had transferred in 1945, he left for Mount Holyoke College in Massachusetts and taught there until 1952. In the meantime he completed *Living Without Being Alive* and started *Con las horas contadas (With Time Running Out)*. The vacations he spent in Mexico during his stay at Mount Holyoke became increasingly important interludes for Cernuda. There he entered into a love affair which made his return to the United States particularly painful. In the fall of 1952, he decided to remain in Mexico where he finished *With Time Running Out* and "Poemas para un cuerpo" ("Poems for a Body") as a separate section in this collection. He also wrote the prose pieces of *Variaciones sobre tema mexicano (Variations on a Mexican Theme)* and taught at the university of Mexico. In 1957, *Estudios sobre poesía española contemporánea (Studies on Contemporary Spanish Poetry)* appeared in Madrid, and in 1958 his book on English poetry, *Pensamiento poético en la lírica inglesa (Poetic Thought in English Lyricism)*, the result of his prolonged study of English poets begun during his stay at Cambridge; the same year saw the publication of the third edition of *Reality and Desire*. In 1960, Cernuda published what was to be the first part of *Poesía y literatura (Poetry and Literature)*, a volume of essays on literary topics. His last book of poetry, *Desolación de la quimera (The Disconsolate Chimera)*, was completed in 1962. In the summer of 1960, he lectured at the University of California, Los Angeles, and in September, 1961, he obtained a post as visiting professor at San Francisco State College, where he taught a course in Spanish poetry and a seminar in style and rhetoric. In September, 1962, he was visiting professor at UCLA through the recommendation of his friend C. P. Otero. The year 1962 also saw the publication of *Poesie di Luis Cernuda*, a beautiful Italian edition of his poetry by Lerici editori, Milan, translated and with an introduction and notes by Francesco T. Montalto. On June 5, 1963, Cernuda returned to Mexico with the intention of coming back to the United States in September, this time to the University of Southern California. In August, 1963, he gave up his position at the University of Southern California, having refused to undergo the medical examination needed to obtain his visa. (In 1960, Vicente Aleixandre had informed him of the death of his surviving sister, confirming his conviction that

it was a family characteristic to die around the age of sixty years.)
Cernuda died November 5, 1963, of a heart attack at the age of
sixty-one.

III   *Cernuda on Cernuda*

Although one could deduce Cernuda's literary biography from the
development of his poetry, such an approach would distort the object
of the poems and lead us to unwarranted extrapolation. It is fortunate,
therefore, that the student of his work is saved from this danger by
Cernuda's "Historial de un libro" ("A Book's History," 1958), a
personal examination of his growth as a poet. In "Palabras antes de
una lectura" ("Words Before a Reading"),[17] published in 1935, he had
already provided an introduction to his work in the form of comments on his understanding of the poet's vision, more particularly his
own. These two texts are invaluable guides to our estimation of his
poetic *cursus vitae* ("development"). *Perfil del aire* seemed to him
"the book of an adolescent, even more adolescent than was my age
upon composing it, . . . but, at the same time, the book of a poet who,
from the point of view of expression, knew more or less where he was
going" (*PL*, 183). The last part of this statement in "History of a Book"
is particularly interesting, for it represents the evaluation by an older
Cernuda of this earliest of his published poems; the essay was written
in 1958 upon the appearance of the last edition he was to see of his
complete poetry. It suggests an unusual steadiness in his creative
course, and, seen from the culmination of the great later poems, an
awareness of his craft striking in a fledgling poet. He was already
searching for straightforward clarity and avoided the fashions of the
day: he would steer true to this course until his last works, secure in
the certainties of his own poetic instinct, while accepting and adapt-
ing only those few ideas which he found useful at different stages of
his career.

   In "Words Before a Reading" Cernuda traces back the conflict at
the basis of his work to the very origins of his poetic awakening: "The
poetic instinct was awakened in me thanks to the more acute perception of reality, experiencing with a deeper echo the beauty and
attraction of the surrounding world."[18] Since then, he recalls, two
opposing forces struggled within him—one toward "reality," the
other against it: ". . . the essence of the poetic problem is constituted by the conflict between reality and desire."[19] He sees the poet's
task as an effort to resolve the conflict through the creation of

moments of equilibrium. Language will dispose the antagonistic forces and give form to the contest. The idea of the poem as a temporary solution gives us from the start two central tenets that will remain true for a large part of Cernuda's poetry: first, there will be a movement within the poem tracing the conflict toward a wedding of such initially opposing forces; second, this newborn equipoise belongs to the development of the poem and to its arrangement of reality along unused paths; it belongs less to the real than to the recreating power of language. The contention between reality and desire seems to arise not from the imperfections possibly inherent in reality, but from those realized in it by the poet's vision and by his subsequent effort to erase them according to his desire. This desire is born of love or the capacity to fall in love, which Cernuda calls the *raiz estética* ("aesthetic root") of poetry, an ability to prolong youth or at least a youthfulness of the spirit. It appears that the greatest defect of reality is its temporality, and the greatest thirst of the poet is for the eternal: "The poet, then, tries to fixate the transitory beauty of the world he perceives, referring it to the invisible world he foresees. . . . "[20] In this effort, even words may sometimes fail the poet, but they are all that he may risk for they contain him. In some way, as in Mallarmé's "Un coup de dés," each poem is a wager against time, with the odds against it, an effort to capture some small portion of truth; and the poem's words may "remain impregnated with the significance that it is only given to the poet to insinuate: the mystery of creation, the hidden beauty of the world"[21]—or, in Mallarmé's own words, "peut-être . . . une constellation."[22]

By 1935, when Cernuda first expressed his poetic credo in "Words Before a Reading," he had written *Perfil del aire* (1924–1927), *Eclogue, Elegy, Ode* (1927–1928), *A River, A Love* (1929), *Forbidden Pleasures* (1931), *Where Oblivion Dwells* (1932–1933), and was concluding *Invocations to the World's Graces* (1934–1935). From the tentative and sometimes precious efforts of *Perfil del aire*, he had gone on to an exercise in craftsmanship with *Eclogue, Elegy, Ode*, where he displayed an easy mastery of technique, coupled with a refusal to conform to fashion that would earn him the repute of haughty disdain which he later struggled long to dispel. His involvement with surrealism in *A River, A Love* and *Forbidden Pleasures* allowed him "a path and form to express in poetry a certain part of that which [he] had not said until then" (*PL*, 187). The movement was for him, personally, more than a literary fashion; it was "a spiritual current in the youth of an epoch before which [he] neither could nor wanted to remain indifferent" (*PL*, 187). The exploration of his deeper self which these poems expressed represented a needed counterpoint to the exercises in virtuosity of his previous work in *Eclogue, Elegy, Ode* where, he said, reversing a statement of Paul Eluard's, "and yet I have never found what I love in what I write" (*PL*, 184). The emotional setback that occasioned the poems of *Where Oblivion Dwells*, although seen later as a moment of humiliation, continued for Cernuda a useful early process of self-exploration. He mentions this particular collection, together with *Eclogue, Elegy, Ode*, as the one he is least pleased with—although not for aesthetic reasons—while accepting the role of the episode in his growth. The next book, *Invocations*, unites his need for a more extensive development of poetic thought with a renewed effort to seize the transitoriness of objects and emotions. Looking back, Cernuda's exacting standards find fault in *Invocations* with moments of diffuseness and strained language. Other critics have seen here some of his better poems of this period.

Although at the beginning of his journey—the first edition of his complete poetry had not yet appeared—Cernuda was already an accomplished poet; he needed now the honing of his craft and the experience that only study and the vicissitudes of life could provide him. By this time, he had read extensively in the Spanish classics and felt a marked preference for Garcilaso. Following the advice of Salinas, he had acquainted himself with the great French poets of the late nineteenth century, Baudelaire, Rimbaud, and Mallarmé, in particular, discovering in the latter poetry that would remain for him of "unequaled beauty" (*PL*, 179). Only later would he come to appreciate the power of Rimbaud's vision while he retained for Baudelaire "a vivid devotion and admiration" (*PL*, 179).

The discovery of Hölderlin, halfway through his writing of *Invocations,* was to be one of the salient moments of his poetic development, but more important still during his residence in England were his reading of English poetry and the new impressions of that country. He found in English poets the conciseness and simplicity he had himself sought for as well as the depth of feeling which he believed the "rhetoricism" of Spanish and French poetry did not allow to emerge: "I learned to avoid, as far as possible, two literary vices known in English, one, as the pathetic fallacy . . . another as purple patch" (*PL*, 200–201). After reading Browning he adopted the dramatic technique that, when needed, allowed him to objectify and give greater amplitude to his poetic thought. Instances of this projective treatment appear in *The Clouds* (1937–1940), begun in Madrid and completed in England, in such poems as "Lazarus"[23] and the trilogy "Resaca en Sansueña" ("Undertow in Sansueña"). It was there also that he began and finished *Como quien espera el alba (Like Someone Waiting for the Dawn*, 1941–1944) in a period which he remembers as one of his most creative: "The autumn, winter and spring from 1941 to 1942 was one of the periods of my life when I felt more impelled by themes and experiences that sought expression in poetry" *(PL*, 202). In spite of such an unusual pace of composition, Cernuda considers this collection one of his favorites. Cernuda looked upon the effect of his readings in English poetry and criticism as a slow cumulative process which did not emphasize any one particular writer or period and which was to continue throughout his life. Some results of such studies became the highly perceptive analyses of *Poetic Thought in English Lyricism* (1958).

He did not, for all that, withdraw his interest from earlier readings in French, German, and classical works. Gide, discovered through Salinas, remained a lifelong absorption. In him he found some answers to the more personal concerns posed by his homosexuality and an echo of the deeply ethical considerations that pervade most of his poetic output. Goethe, Rilke, and Hölderlin continued to engross him, through the quality of their lives as poets as much as through their work. His interest in ancient philosophy was rekindled while at Mount Holyoke by his reading of Diels' *Fragmente der Vorsokratiker* and Burnet's *Early Greek Philosophy*. Not surprisingly, when one thinks of Cernuda's anxiety before the flow of time, Heraclitus touched in him particularly responsive chords, while the beauty of ancient myths remained in his mind pristine as at first. As he says in "El poeta y los mitos" ("The Poet and Myths") from *Ocnos*, in that world "poetry, vivifying it as fire does the log, transcended the real."[24]

The effort to achieve the power of encompassing temporality and recreating a reality that would do so stood at the basis of Cernuda's poetic endeavor; together with a constant striving for verbal limpidity and conciseness, this preoccupation was to continue fundamentally unaltered to his death. In this latter respect, as early as upon the publication of the first edition of *Reality and Desire*, he reworked the poems of *Perfil del aire* and changed the title of the collection to *Primeras poesías (First Poems)*, disliking, he says, any of its clever or precious connotations. Reflecting upon his work from the vantage point of "History of a Book," he found that much of it did not satisfy his standard of economy and clarity. It was the "nakedness" of Reverdy's verse that first attracted him, for instance, although his taste for the French poet diminished considerably later on. He abandoned rhyme as early as 1929 and turned toward muted rhythms, allowing the sentence to bear its own cadence together with that of the individual line. He sought as well to compose his poems upon a solid experiential base conducive to precision of contour and of expression.

Always shunning facile mannerisms or fashions, driven by a constant search for directness, Cernuda remained to the end attached to his early ideal of the poet as compositor of a more vibrant, more serene world. This world is evoked as the echo of a higher, superseding harmony, not unlike that of the Neoplatonists, wherein the spirit belongs. Nevertheless, and in spite of the esoteric overtones of a number of his compositions, Cernuda's poetry remains rooted in reality, albeit as a *materia prima* ("raw material") to be reshaped. Similarly, his concept of love, though capable of expanding to quasi-mystical proportions, finds its source at the sensual, erotic core of his being, to which it always returns. As we hope to show, these extremes are complementary aspects of Cernuda's ethical lyricism.

CHAPTER 2

First Poetry

I *Introduction*

E VERY form seemed to gather under the name and every name
to rouse the form, with that pristine exactness of a creation:
the exterior and interior corresponded and conformed to one another
as between lovers the desire of one and the surrender of the other.
And your body listened to the light."[1]

This passage is taken from "La Luz" ("The Light"), one of the most
striking pieces in *Ocnos*. The entire prose poem describes a moment
of openness to the world. Such a receptive stance is in Cernuda the
Terminus ad quem of his poetic activity and represents but one of
his responses to reality, although the one he sought constantly to
achieve. The other two are, as we shall see later, rejection and
withdrawal. Although more frequent, they are not of as great an
intrinsic significance since they constitute, ideally, points of departure toward the spiritual communion described in "The Light."

The poem is a second-person narrative in which the speaker recalls
the effect that the morning light by the sea had on his naked body and
on his mind. He felt light penetrating him, creating harmony, and
eliciting a sensation of unity with the world. Light at this moment
appeared a testimony of the divine, although it also brought the
anguish of anticipated death. Does the body become light after
death? Should it not be so, the speaker assures himself, your body has
accumulated enough light "to illuminate . . . death"(*O*, 162). The
portion quoted earlier concludes the first paragraph of the poem and
describes the instant of pure interpenetration of light and body. It
seems an agreement of forms, of thought to matter, similar to the
embrace of two lovers.

We notice immediately here the stress on the shaping function of
language, the two principal elements of the initial clause—"form"

and "name"—being conjoined to one another "with that pristine exactness of a creation." From this statement on the sources we proceed to a simile introducing the presence of man in general— loving couple—and the happy correspondence of desire and its satisfaction. The last sentence brings to bear the force of the event on the poet's past ecstatic self. In this last image[2] there occurs as the result of the light penetrating the reclining form a corresponding mutual interpenetration of the senses of touch, sight, and hearing. All limits within are erased, as are those between world and body.

This passage contains also some thoughts that remain important throughout Cernuda's work and to which we shall have frequent occasion to return. There is first the very idea we have mentioned of openness to and union with the real, more often than not an un-realized possibility. Second, we note that the communion itself is immediately seen in terms of gratified erotic desire. An explicit statement on this point appears in the last piece of *Ocnos*, "El acorde" ("The Consonance"), which deals precisely with the same type of occurrence: ". . . you can perceive, want, or understand nothing unless it enters in you first through sex, from there to the heart and later to the mind" (*O*, 193). Third, religious connotations, although not explicit, surround the statement with mystical reminis-cences which will recur in many such instances. Cernuda generally rejects traditional religion, and his intuitive sympathy with mysticism is largely owing to its Gnostic or Neoplatonic components.[3] Linked with this point is the fourth important implication whereby language is perceived at the source of creation. For in his merging with reality the poet sees "the word"[4] at the origin of things as it is at the origin of his own re-creation of the cosmos, and he discovers therein the essence of his poetry. His most satisfying efforts are thus, for him, tied to his capacity for openness to the world.

Fortunately, the excellence of Cernuda's work is not dependent upon such experiences. He was well aware of the difficulties inherent in the communication of moments of heightened awareness; such experiences, he believes, generally escape us ". . . through our incapacity to explore them, and that was my situation upon writing the prose poem 'The Consonance' " (*PL*, 208). It continues to be true that Cernuda's conception of cosmic desire as the mainspring of his work is a lasting one—witness the title of his complete poems—and also that this desire has a strong sexual component. In "History of a Book" he remarks on this eroticism "at the source": "Around the age of fourteen, and the coincidence with the sexual awakening of puberty should here be mentioned, I made my first attempt to write verse" (*PL*, 177–78).

Cernuda's longing for plenitude, for the abolition of the basic duality world-poet, is but one of the three central dispositions recurring in his poems. Another, opposite point of view, perhaps the most frequent, is a rejection of reality or rather the awareness of the chasm existing between the world as it is and the world desire seeks. The defects of reality are those that mark its distance from the realm of the ideal: incoherence and temporality. The third position is one of withdrawal into the seclusion of a privileged environment, a Virgilian *locus amoenus*[5] ("idyllic spot") wherein tranquillity and at least a partial harmony may be found. This Eden need not be a particular place, such as the "Hidden Garden" of *First Poems*[6] or the child's room protected from the rain in "La tormenta" ("The Storm") of *Ocnos;* it can also occur as a special moment of the day in which the landscape seems to reveal itself in new accord.

In Cernuda's earliest poetry the opposing elements are still quite clearly defined as reality and the poet. Soon, specific aspects of the world will stand out, generally adding their weight to its antagonistic, irretrievable aspect: man, social impositions, time. The inner man in his turn also discovers allies in the contest: love, poetry, solitude, sometimes light. But these forces contain as well the germ of their opposite; love creates the possibility of loss or oblivion, poetry often reveals the insufficiency of language, and solitude may turn into alienation. In this chapter we shall examine the first phase of Cernuda's poetry, up to *Invocations*, with some emphasis on his three possible attitudes toward the duality world-man mentioned above: reaching for plenitude, rejection of reality, withdrawal to a privileged *locus*.

II First Poems *and Eclogue, Elegy, Ode*

Cernuda's early poetry reveals a young man of delicate sensibility, with a fine ear for the musicality of his language, an already accomplished craftsman. His own testimony in this respect thirty years later refers both to the certainties of his technique and the indefiniteness of his emotions.[7] He has not yet adopted a firm stand toward the world his senses discover, although he is aware of the disparity between the form it assumes and that which he wishes to see in it. His answer to this disparity is frequently to attempt a withdrawal into his inner world where, more often than not, he is met by the unsatisfac-

tory vagueness of his own desires. This recoiling will often lead to
frustration: in Poem XVIII of *First Poems* the adolescent appears at
first secure within four walls from the harshness of the outside
world—"walls, nothing else./Lifeless, noiseless,/Without harsh
words,/Life lies inert"—only to find the solitude ultimately oppressive: "But nobody sighs./My hands have nothing/To hold but tears.
Silence;/Darkness trembling; nothing."[8] Only later will a pregnant
idleness come to replace mere indolence and tedium as the necessary
meditative repose preparatory to creation. At the other extreme,
there appears the response of narcissism whereby, not able to find an
adequate object of desire in the outside world, he turns toward
himself through the image of Narcissus: "In an enchanted dream/
Beyond insurmountable space/Narcissus in love/Enjoys his irretrievable beauty."[9]

Time, the most elusive aspect of reality for Cernuda, and the most
destructive, will prove a major challenge from the beginning. One of
the young poet's responses to the transitoriness of experience is to
create objects immune to it. Thus, in "Homenaje" ("Homage") we
see a clear opposition between the enduring song and the mortal
singer—in this case Fray Luis:

> Time, harshly accumulating
> Oblivion of the singer, annihilates him not;
> Ever young his voice throbs and vibrates,
> And goes on singing to the world of men.
>
> But the mortal flight so sweet, where
> Has it desperately fled? Undone vigor,
> Imperious marble hides it
> In a somber melancholy repose.

(RD, 27)

Poetry may thus provide a measure of durability, often exalting
elements of nature, mythical or real, to abstract them from the flow of
time. Such an element is the young god of "Oda" ("Ode"): "And his
form reveals/A world eternally portended." The god merely rushes
by; not only are the accustomed demands of passion inappropriate in
such a presence, even desire at its most ideal is too coarse. The divine
figure inevitably returns to its abode when " . . . to the bank nearby,
to the light water,/After its strange image the form jumps" as a
newborn Narcissus. The image of imperishable form plunging into
the slowly flowing water "identical to itself and fugitive" widens the

chasm between the creations of desire and those offered by time; the water, here understood in its immediate metaphorical value of pure temporality—"identical to itself"—does not ultimately hold the young god's shape:[10] "The blest body escapes nigh on the wing/ Leaving the thicket/For the purple delight of the sky" (*RD*, 35–38). The double abstraction from duration possible through the choice of poetic object—here a divine being—and a poetic effect—in this case increased by the skillful use of a stately, classical meter—may combine at times to create a present inured to its past or future occasions. In the "Egloga" ("Eclogue"), although on the point of disarray, a fragile, Edenic present is sustained for a moment within the secluded tranquillity of a garden:

> The present endures,
> Forgotten in its dream,
> Expanded in agile foreshortening.
> Delight. Sweetly,
> Without desire or insistence
> The hesitating instant is asleep.

Dusk will soon allow dark uncertainty to penetrate and abolish the calm contours of the instant: "The sky no longer sings, / Nor does its celestial eternity attend/The light and the roses/Rather the nocturnal horror of things" (*RD*, 29–31).

The unavoidable transitoriness of things is at the source of the poet's disillusionment with a deceptive reality; it represents another element contributing to the inner void and consequent *hastío* ("disgust") already present in his earliest work and increasingly frequent thereafter. Cernuda's concern with time has in fact been regarded as the axis of his poetry,[11] the very origin of the reality-desire disjunction. Much of our own attention will bear upon this question, although, as we have already pointed out and hope to make clear subsequently, we only see it as one facet of the broader world-poet opposition—the "world" being of course understood not merely as the world of things but also that of man.

A further consequence of this awareness is the poet's inclination to solitude. Just as unproductive indolence may also become fruitful *ocio* ("idleness"), so does solitude bring either solace or despair according to whether it is at the origin of poetic activity or results merely from a clash with circumstance. Only in solitude does the *locus amoenus* (idyllic spot) hold its spell, and it will be recreated, its

mystery cast into words only in meditative retirement. But a fruitless
withdrawal transforms seclusion into imprisonment; walls, no longer
protective, close in on the youth, while beauty remains unattainable.
Thus, the concluding lines of Poem XXII: "What absence, what
delirium/Made of beauty an alien?/Your bland youth, in the
sorrow/Of an empty white paper" (*RD*, 23).

There are as yet too many uncertainties, and passion is still too
diffuse to populate solitude. Desire is not the powerfully focussed
energy it will become later, strong enough to illuminate the emptiest
confines. But the young poet sees in love's bonds those that har-
monize the cosmos, as the force of desire holds together his poetic
universe. "Love Moves the World" (from *First Poems*, Poem X)
describes precisely this correspondence in love of the outer and inner
worlds. The poem begins with an assertion of love as the world's
motive force and the weak echo that it elicits within the poet: "Love
moves the world/Resting lost/To the gaze. And this/Tenderness
without use." Stanza two, as it follows the waning of daylight—
"Already the lights begin/The daily exodus"—prepares us for the
arrival in the next stanza of the "angel" of inspiration, the poet's inner
light. Now the "Tenderness without use" of the first stanza becomes a
worthy response; desire shaped by language turns into a love that is
the true inner echo of the initial cosmic harmony: "The word
awaited/Illuminates the spheres;/A new love reappears/To the pros-
trate sense." In the final stanza the poem asserts its own significance
as the third necessary step in the descending flow of inspiration: "The
dreams, forgotten,/Are borne away by the winds./Repose.
Transformed/Tenderness is cast off" (*RD*, 16).

This composition is an early expression of the poet's coming to
terms with external reality through the agency of his poetry. It
establishes the poem as a temporary solution to disjunction; its inner
movement takes terms initially separate, in that "tenderness" is an
inadequate echo to cosmic love, toward the stronger response that
the work of language itself will create, a corresponding "new love."
The development belongs to the poem itself, not to the circumstance;
in fact, the poem is not simply its necessary agent, but its only
possible expression. In this respect Cernuda's own appreciation of his
early work comes to mind once more: certainly the poet's youth
occasionally allows an overingenious metaphor to penetrate—in this
instance, the image of the angel who "Sought a sonnet/Amid his
feathers"—and there remain some emotional imprecisions, but by
and large he already had his craft well in hand.

III *The Surrealist Moment*

Not only was surrealism inevitable for Cernuda because, as a young poet open to foreign influences and having traveled to France, he was bound to become familiar with this most important poetic movement of the day; of greater consequence for him, it proclaimed sociopolitical tenets that answered his own rebelliousness while sanctioning dreams and other elements from the unconscious as legitimate poetic material. Surrealism was the experience he needed precisely at this moment in order to gain the confidence with which to plunge within himself and redefine with clarity what had been, until then, diffuse aspirations.

The unifying experience that would abolish distances, object of Cernuda's striving, had been intuited earlier by Breton: "Everything leads one to believe that there exists a certain point of the spirit from which life and death, the real and the imaginary, the past and the future, the communicable and the incommunicable, the high and the low, cease to be perceived contradictorily."[12] In this rejection of dualism, both writers refuse to look for the coalescing principle in any traditionally religious beyond. It is attainable within the poet should the quest not be impeded by reality. That is why reality is either rejected in many of these poems or remolded according to desire in a few.

At a more immediate level, Cernuda's agreements with surrealism implied, in the words of C. B. Morris, "the determination to be true to himself at all costs. To have stifled his hostility to 'fetid laws' and 'hollow realities' would have betrayed [his] moral rectitude."[13] In terms of his craft, he was never to embrace wholly the technique of automatism; although, as he tells us in "History of a Book," he did write a large number of the poems in *A River, A Love* and *Forbidden Pleasures* without corrections and in two short bursts of intense creativity, he did not surrender entirely to the dictates of his unconscious. Another of the surrealists' doctrines more in agreement with his own tendencies was their preference for a colloquial, understated style. Oblivion, rebellion, dying, all may be treated poetically in the most straightforward tones, even in lines that are intentionally unmelodic. Also at this time he leaves aside altogether any concern with rhyme and adopts free verse: ". . .I had had a certain difficulty in using free verse; with the impulse that animated me then, the difficulty was overcome, . . .I eschewed rhyme, consonant or assonant, and hardly since then have I ever used the first" (*PL,* 188).

Thus, from the point of view of his search for a unifying vision, as well as from that of revolt, Cernuda's encounter with surrealism confirmed him in his endeavor and encouraged him to seek further. Nevertheless, the strong emotional upheaval that he underwent at a time immediately preceding *A River, A Love* and still haunting him when writing *Forbidden Pleasures* turned these poems for the most part into expressions of frustration and anger. Very seldom do we perceive that quality of calm receptiveness which also belongs to the surrealist attitude.

While the predominant mood of the thirty poems of *A River, A Love* (1929) and the twenty-six of *Forbidden Pleasures* (1931) is one of rejection, a small number of compositions leave a door open to an imaginary setting where the clashing oppositions that daily confront the poet disappear. The poem "Nevada," for instance, with the resonance of a few words erects a dreamlike, nearly ideal scenery: "The transparent nights/Disclose dream lights on the waters,/ Reflect the pure holidaylike/Constellated roof-tops." The cold chastity of snow infuses the darkness with light, leaving only the purity of line wherein all oppositions are resolved: "Tears smile,/Sadness is winged," and heaviness takes flight: "The railroads are named after birds" (*PC*, 12–13). Desire also, together with dreaming, may smooth out asperities and resolve antagonisms. The surrealists saw in it the power to "unrealize": "Thus, in order to be possessed by desire, the world must be deprived of the hardness of its physical structure, woman of the hardness of her conscious structure; dream unrealizes [*déréalise*] the world. . . ."[14] And so in the poem "Los marineros son las alas del amor" ("Sailors are the Wings of Love") of *Forbidden Pleasures:*

> If a sailor is the sea,
> Blond loving sea whose presence is a chant,
> I do not want the city made of gray dreams;
> I want only to go to the sea to be submerged,
> Boat without pole star,
> Body without pole star to drown in its blond light.

> (*RD*, 72)

The dissolving power of the sea affords the possibility of shedding both rational and physical constraints, of returning to the unifying origins of love.

When escape is impossible, the poet is faced with a disparate universe standing inexorably between him and any possible fulfillment. From angered refusal in *A River, A Love* to the more resigned, though not less denunciatory tone of *Forbidden Pleasures,* Cernuda's indictment of social man pervades this poetry. To express his experience of alienation, a broad range of images is brought into play including one of the poet as a ghost among men and another of the world as a prison. Existence is a living death, reason either destroyed or decaying.

In the poem "Telarañas cuelgan de la razón"[15] ("Cobwebs are Hanging from the Mind"), the mind is first presented as fallen into disuse, caught in a burned-out body, consumed by the holocaust of love: "Cobwebs are hanging from the mind/In a landscape turned to ash./The hurricane of love has passed." In the wake of this disaster there remains no sign of life. The lover has been destroyed, split asunder by the sole appearance of the beloved, the substance of his life draining away or evaporating like "drops of water when a sea dries up." The mind shattered, its scattered pieces must be reassembled as best one can, emptied life gathered before it may be slowly replenished with dreams and desire. The loved one remains afar: ". . . cruel as the day;/Daylight, that light that tightly hugs a sad wall,/A wall, can't you understand?/A wall in front of which I stand alone" (*PC*, 22–23). The effectiveness of the poem resides in the careful metaphorical opposition between mind and body, land and water, water and burning light. No solution is reached; the last image is one of arid imprisonment.

Deprived of love, his *aqua vitae,* the poet is like a ghost, wandering aimlessly. The entire world is a cell. In "Tu pequeña figura" ("Your Small Figure") the speaker searches in a vast, ruined universe for the smallest sign of life: "You seek over the earth a hoary shuddering/While the walls, with their ancient ivy/Grow slowly over the dusk." A gray sameness pervades the world of man, life slowly draining away: "Listen to the water, listen to the rain, listen to the storm;/That is your life:/Liquid lament flowing amid like shadows". (*RD*, 77). Man's monstrous refusal to see or to understand makes the poet's existence a living death. The blindness of "the others" is like a fog reaching out to dissolve him, negate him to himself. This process is strikingly rendered in "En medio de la multitud" ("In the Midst of the Multitude"):

Empty, I walked aimlessly through the city. Strange people passed me by without seeing me. As it brushed against me a body melted with a gentle whisper. I walked on and on.

I could not feel my feet. I wanted to take them in my hand, and I could not find my hands; I wanted to shout, and I could not find my voice. The mist enveloped me.

Life weighed on me like remorse; I wanted to cast out my life. But it was impossible, for I was dead and wandered among the dead.[16]

With Baudelaire in "Anywhere Out of the World," Cernuda could also say: "It seems to me I would always feel well wherever I don't happen to be. . . ."[17] Rebellion is one answer when such escape is not possible; but rebellion can only lead to frustration. The poet wanders aimlessly, a ghost in a world of ghosts. The protective walls of the secluded garden in *First Poems* close in on him in *A River, A Love* and *Forbidden Pleasures.* But toward the end of this last collection a mood of calm resignation begins to appear. The walls are still there, the multitude is as impenetrable as always, but the poet has learned that some things may retain their value and that they are worth seeking. In any case, the past is now seen more equably: "I saw my youth neither gained nor lost,/I saw my body distant, as alien/As myself, there in an alien hour" ("Veía sentado" ["I Saw Seated"]; *RD*, 82). "I've Come to See," the last poem of *Forbidden Pleasures,* looks toward the future with some acceptance, perhaps even hope:

> *I've come to see death*
> And its funny net for hunting butterflies,
> *I've come to wait for you,*
> My arms somewhat in the air,
> I've come I don't know why;
> One day I opened my eyes: I have come.
>
> (*PC*, 32–33)

Death remains, though somewhat diminished; love may some day be possible again.

In summary, while the surrealist moment seems to have been for Cernuda one of intense personal suffering, poetically it helped him to liberate himself from constraints of form and broadened the expressive range of his voice. He learned to use concrete detail to greater effect and moved closer to the strong simplicity of his later poetry through the deliberately colloquial tone of many poems. In the light of his total development, although it did not produce any of his greater compositions, Cernuda's experiment with surrealism remains crucial, and the quality of his work even then is certainly comparable to that of the best poets of the period. His own words on the movement are an apt summary of its importance to his poetry: "It had already afforded its benefit, bringing to light what laid in my unconscious, that which until its oncoming remained within me in blindness and silence" (*PL*, 192).

IV   Where Oblivion Dwells and Invocations

A.   Where Oblivion Dwells

In "History of a Book" Cernuda introduces his comments on *Where Oblivion Dwells* with a reference to the impact that the reading of Bécquer had on him at that time: "The reading of Bécquer, or rather the rereading of the same [the title of the collection, "Donde habite el olvido," is a line from the "Rima LXVI" by Bécquer], set me toward a new poetic vision and expression" (*PL*, 192). Looking back on these poems, he finds them unsatisfactory not from the aesthetic but from the ethical point of view. He says of the experience at their source: "The story was sordid, and so I saw it after having overcome it; in it my reaction had been too candid (my spiritual development was slow, also in the love experience) and too cowardly" (*PL*, 192). For our purposes, we shall examine *Where Oblivion Dwells*, as well as *Invocations*, mainly in terms of their formal significance; not because of Cernuda's unhappiness with their biographical content but because, while the importance of the surrealist works resided to a great extent in their role as experiments of self-discovery, that of these poems consists in the development of his art. Furthermore, they deal mainly with the loss of love at a level which transcends the personal. That particular love experience had constituted—erroneously, Cernuda later thinks—a possibility of achieving plenitude. Its loss is often seen as the loss of this possibility.

The sixteen numbered poems of *Where Oblivion Dwells* present one of the most unremitting indictments of love in recent Spanish literature. In the last poem of the collection, unnumbered and titled, "Los fantasmas del deseo" ("The Phantoms of Desire"), love has become so depersonalized that it is seen as an expression of the native earth choosing the poet as its spokesman: "Well I know now that it is

you/Who dictate this form and this yearning to me." The composition
in an apt rendition of the poet's occasional transcendence of personal
emotion even at the level of the most immediate desire; he is left
"With this desire that appears to be mine and is not even mine,/But
the desire of all." In this pessimistic frame of mind, however, the
realization comes too late: "Earth, earth and desire/A lost form" (*RD*,
100–101). From the vantage point of this final composition, it is
possible to understand other poems of the collection in the light in
which Cernuda himself saw some of his surrealist pieces, as ways of
dealing with painful experiences: ". . . one way of satisfying them,
exorcising them, would be to lend them expression" (*PL*, 185).

Where Oblivion Dwells first appeared in 1934, although it is dated
1932–1933. "Where Oblivion Dwells" was Bécquer's suggestion for
his own epitaph in "Rima LXVI," line sixteen; in Cernuda's use, the
tone is set by the prose epigraph which says in part: "What remains of
the joys and pains of love when it disappears? Nothing, or worse than
nothing; there remains the remembrance of an oblivion. . . . The
following pages are the remembrance of an oblivion" (*RD*, 86), and by
the first poem, strongly reminiscent of Bécquer's "Rima." This poem
contains the kernel of the disillusionment with love and the yearning
for escape from a despairing present which mark the entire collection. We quote it in full:

> Where oblivion dwells,
> In vast gardens without a dawn;
> Where I shall only be
> The memory of a stone, buried among nettles,
> Over which the wind escapes its insomnias.
>
> Where my name will leave the body it names
> In the arms of the centuries
> Where desire will not exist.
>
> In those great regions where the terrible
>   angel of love
> Will not hide his steellike wing in my breast,
> Smiling, full of aerial grace,
> While the anguish grows.
>
> There where this longing—which requires a
>   master in its own image,
> Submitting its life to another life,
> No horizon except other eyes, face to face—
> There, where this longing will end.

> Where sorrow and joy will be only words,
> Heaven and earth native to remembrance;
> Where, without knowing it, I shall finally
>   be free,
> Dispersed in mist, an absence,
> Absence, slight as the flesh of a child.
>
> There, there far away;
> Where oblivion dwells.

(PC, 37)

It would be useful here to recall Bécquer's poem, following, as it were, Cernuda's own suggestion. His allusion is to the last four lines of "Rima LXVI": "Where there will be a solitary stone/with no inscription whatever,/where oblivion dwells/there my tomb will be." Bécquer's poem traces the journey of the lover's soul from "Whence do I come from? Seek the most horrible and rugged of paths," to "Where am I going: Cross the darkest and saddest of deserts;/valley of eternal snows and of eternal melancholy mists."[18] We see immediately that "Where Oblivion Dwells" is not really a paraphrase of the earlier poem, but rather that the "Rima" constitutes its point of departure, one which must be kept in mind by the reader if he wants to experience the full force of the later composition. Actually, Cernuda's poem constitutes an answer to Bécquer's. The latter contains two implied injunctions: "If you want to know whence I come, seek . . .", "if you want to know where I am going, cross . . ."; Cernuda's answer is that his own past itinerary was so painful that he wishes for the "valley of eternal snows and of eternal melancholy mists"; this will be for him a deliverance, an "Absence, slight as the flesh of a child."

The suppression in "Where Oblivion Dwells" of any direct reference to the speaker's wishes—"I want to go where . . ." or "I would like to go . . ."—results in a concentration of effect, giving greater emphasis to the object of the wish while it illustrates an important thought of the poem: the suppression of desire. Paradoxically, the absent wish becomes more insistent in the mind of the reader who is led to "fill in" the missing statement. This technique by implication is pursued throughout the poem in that the unmentioned point of origin—"Where I am"—appears in detail, described in terms of the desired point of arrival—"Where I would like to be . . ."; "here" is seen in terms of "there" and acquires, in fact, greater

importance. Thus, instead of a picture of the end of suffering, we have
one of suffering in terms of its cessation.

There is a progression in the poem as may be easily seen from the
fact that the distance from "here" to "there" has increased in the last
two lines: "There, there, far away;/Where oblivion dwells." The
initial lines describe the vastness of that zone: "Where oblivion
dwells,/In vast gardens without a dawn," but not its remoteness. This
movement proceeds in three main steps: the first one includes lines 1
to 8, itself divisible into four aspects of the "where." Lines 1 and 2 are
a general metaphorical description of the abode of death; lines 3 to 5
pertain to the speaker's wish for disappearance therein where his
death will be forgotten and even his tombstone will be buried. The
general impression conveyed is one of total, long-forgotten death,
when even the wind ignores the lost, anonymous marker of the
speaker's existence. Lines 6 and 7 reiterate this idea through the
separation of the body and its name, that is, a loss of identity is
wished for; we notice that it is the name, not the spirit, which is seen
as separable from the body. This suggests that the essence which the
speaker is concerned with is entirely physical. The last line of this first
part—"Where desire will not exist"—is a further specification of
meaningful attributes. From line 6 on, in terms of increasing significance for the speaker, such attributes are "name," "body," and
"desire."

While the first moment of the poem describes the speaker's
yearning in general, through increasingly specific terms within this
generality, the second one goes to the heart of the problem and
concerns the disillusionment and pain of love. A renewed development is introduced by "In those great regions . . . ," an echo of "In
vast gardens. . . ." Lines 9 to 12 describe the effect of love through a
series of oxymoronlike contradictory expressions: "Terrible angel,"
"steellike wing," "grace/anguish." The opposition of terms used to
describe the circumstances of love emphasizes the fascination and
horror it produces as well as the helplessness of the victim. "Will not
hide his steellike wing in my breast" is particularly striking as an
image of the frustrated yearning of love—concretely, the steel wing is
the trapped, beating heart—which wants to transcend the human and
cannot, especially for Cernuda whose concept of it was so thoroughly
physical. As we shall see below, by its very nature such desire is fated
to unfulfillment.

This idea of "Eros imprisoned" is most explicitly rendered in
strophe four, where the flaw at love's center appears to be its

narcissistic nature.[19] The gradual emergence of the unbridgeable gap between "here" and "there" was begun with "those" in "those great regions . . ." and is pursued now with "There where this longing. . . ." A narrowing circle of limitations is defined through the gradations of "its own image," "life . . . life," "face to face." The expressions that accompany these increasingly concrete oppositions likewise describe a movement from willed action—"requires"—to submission—"submitting"—to prison—"No horizon." Concurrently, the sustained duality negates the yearned-for union of lover and loved one. In the search for the image, we find the barrier of one's eyes, seeking.

The fifth and sixth stanzas conclude the design; while there is a return to the generality of the initial situation,[20] there are also more intimate connotations sustaining the flow from the preceding lines. Echoes of the opening underline the transformations that those initial statements have undergone; to "I shall only" answers "I shall finally be free"; "Heaven and earth native to remembrance" was "The memory of a stone"; "Where my name will leave the body . . ." is now "sorrow and joy will be only words"—the Spanish has "nombres" ("nouns") for "words". Last, the freedom sought for, "Absence, slight as the flesh of a child," implies that this land "Where oblivion dwells" is akin to the child's world of innocence.

The two concluding lines complete the distancing of that world from this as the final stage of the progression: "In vast gardens," "In those great regions," "There, there far away." The last line is now pregnant with the connotations of the entire poem and has become more precisely not merely "nowhere" but "nowhen." In fact, all the spatial references of the poem are really temporal ones, either by implication or explicitly so: "oblivion" itself is a time referent as are "memory" and "remembrance"; so are "without a dawn," "In the arms of the centuries," and also "name" which is our temporal identity label; the remembrance of childhood at the end also suggests a desire to transform time. In this sense, the impossibility of finding erotic fulfillment goes beyond the narcissistic elements of the search to show that it is inevitable because desire by its nature wants to transcend time and is born of that which is temporal. Furthermore, Cernuda's decision to delineate his "here and now" in terms of "there and never," as it were, actually shows that suffering is forever inescapable since we can conceive of death or heaven or that "Absence, slight as . . ." only in terms of our life. The imprisonment pursues us beyond the grave.

The two ideas that constitute the axis of this poem also inform the entire collection and remain central throughout Cernuda's work; they are, as mentioned above, a negative view of the world—born of the disillusionment of love—and the wish to escape its confines. We see, however, that they represent but one moment of that oscillation of the poet toward reality and away from it, which we established earlier as his most characteristic tendencies. Cernuda here sees the world through love or its insufficiency.

Love, and now its passing, have so totally possessed him that he can conceive of it only as an overpowering elemental force. The sea will frequently become its correlative image and provide two metaphorical alternatives: it may elicit the desire to plunge into it, to become one with it as if it were the very essence of love, such as in Poem II: "I contemplate its waves and I would like to drown myself, / Desperately wanting / To descend. . . . / To the bottom of love itself that no man has seen" (*RD*, 88); or it may represent the only possible response to his own all-encompassing yearning, the ideal, versatile, and absolute lover: "The sea is an oblivion / A song, a single lip; / The sea is a lover, / Faithful answer to desire" (Poem VI; *RD*, 90). Love, of course, supersedes man while giving him the only true glimpse of life:

> It is not love that dies
> But we ourselves.
> . . . .
> Only he lives who has
> Always before him the eyes of his dawn,
> Only he lives who kisses
> That angel's body love constructed.
>
> (Poem XII; *PC*, 41)

Man, without it, is but emptiness: "Living and not living, dead and not dead; / Neither earth nor sky, neither body nor spirit. / I am the echo of something" (Poem III; *RD*, 88–89).

Utter surrender, incapable of providing an adequate response, leads inevitably to utter despair and from such imprisonment only death can free the poet: "No, I would not want to return, / But to die even more, / To tear out a shadow, / To forget a forgetting" (Poem XI; *RD*, 94–95), or, in Poem V, "I want death between my hands" (*RD*, 90). The real, deprived of love, its inmost essence, becomes a meaningless void or a prison: "Under the iron sky / Bitterness grows leaves, / Heavy within the chains / That sustain life" (Poem VIII; *RD*,

92). Death, or oblivion, offers a possible abstraction from the temporal, freedom from its chains. Childhood, although closer to nothingness and therefore to liberation, is in *Where Oblivion Dwells* already limited by existence: "I was a child / Prisoner within changing walls" (Poem VII; *RD*, 91). Only earliest infancy, when man is mere potential, provides the precious, delicate detachment where desire and peace may coexist:

> You were tender desire, insinuating cloud,
> You lived with the air amid friendly bodies
> You breathed without form, you smiled
>   without voice,
> Inspired remnant of invisible spirit.
>
> (Poem XIV; *RD*, 96)

Although ceaselessly invoked, such an inviolate Eden[21] remains forever unattainable, unless death itself should provide it. But the more resigned outlook expressed in the last poem of the collection— "The Phantoms of Desire" (see above, page 37)—allows some aspects of reality more resistant to time to manifest themselves. It is chiefly with these that Cernuda's next book of poetry is concerned.

B.   Invocations

After the emotional debacle witnessed in *Where Oblivion Dwells*, *Invocations* seems generally to express the poet's effort to turn his eyes away from the most painful aspects of his experience, to find still "untainted" poetic material, as it were, within and without himself. The collection was written in 1934–1935 and bore the title, *Invocaciones a las gracias del mundo* (*Invocations to the World's Graces*), until the 1958 edition of *Reality and Desire*, when as Cernuda did for *Perfil del aire*, he changed it to its shorter form. Looking back upon these poems with his accustomed severity, Cernuda found some of them less than satisfactory. But, whereas in *Where Oblivion Dwells* it was the experience behind the poetry that disturbed him, in the later collection his criticisms pertained more to the work itself. His wish to "expand [his] limits of the poetic experience," he thinks, led him to "ramble not a little, particularly at the beginning of certain poems in said collection. One notices also, in the tone of the same, some pomposity" (*PL*, 193). Actually he was reacting to poets of his generation who "had lost perhaps the sense of what composition is." The broadening of the limits of his poetry

responded to that of his experience. Together with a growing
confidence in his art, this led him to believe that "at that time [he] felt
capable (forgive the presumption) to say everything in the poem,
before the petty limitation of that which in the years immediately
preceding was called 'pure' poetry."

As the title itself suggests, *Invocations* represents a moment in
Cernuda's poetry when he determinedly sought to move toward a
renewed awareness of that stable reality which it is given to the
inspired poet to perceive in fleeting instances. But, what is perhaps
more important, his poems here suggest less an effort to transmit his
vision than to create one, to establish it through language. And as in
Poem I of *Where Oblivion Dwells* only in the reference to our limited
horizon can a broader one be understood. Thus, throughout *Invocations* the opposition between our present society and the poet's pagan
ideal repeatedly issues forth. Seldom in contemporary poetry has
such a bitter denunciation of social man been expressed as that in "La
gloria del poeta" ("The Poet's Glory"):

> Men, you know them, my brother;
> See how they straighten their invisible crown
> While they disappear in the shadow, wives at
>   their arm,
> Load of unconscious sufficiency,
> Bearing at a discreet distance from their breast,
> As Catholic priests the shape of their god,
> The sons obtained in a few minutes that were
>   stolen from sleep
> To dedicate them to cohabitation, in the dense
>   conjugal darkness
> Of their lairs piled one on top of the other,
>
> . . . .
> Contemplate their strange brains
> Attempting to erect, son by son, a complicated
>   edifice of sand
> That may negate with a grim livid brow the refulgent
>   peace of the stars.

These are, however, substanceless copies of what man really is, of
what the poet knows himself to be, although he is here condemned to
erect his own unheeded world from which death is the only liberation: "For the vain task of words tires me." Man is caught in a social
prison of his own devising that insulates him from nature—

"Demanding shelter for the child chained under the divine sun"—
and from any awareness of the unity beyond. To sustain the empty
strictures of family life, he has constructed an equally rigid and empty
religious pantheon—"See how they abandon their work on the
seventh authorized day." The poet's enterprise is illusory, and if
there is to be a true, meaningful song, only in death will it be born:
"Death only/Can make the promised melody resound"(*RD*, 113–15).

This bitterness is excluded from the other poems of *Invocations*.
Such anger turns against the poet, as it does finally in this poem, and
closes all doors between him and that which in nature, if not society,
reveals the beautiful and the lasting. A calm perspective is only
achieved through greater objectivity. In "Soliloquio del farero"
("Soliloquy of the Lighthousekeeper"), Cernuda uses for the first
time the technique of personification—which shall acquire such
importance in his later poetry—to objectify and explore the effects of
consciously sought solitude, an aspect of his own poetic condition.
Here, solitude is preferable to commerce with humanity not wholly
because of its intrinsic present fruitfulness, but rather because of the
speaker's disenchantment with society. The basic metaphorical structure of the poem as a movement from light to darkness to light reveals
the alterations undergone by solitude. For the child such solitude was
possessed of a true inner radiance:

> As a child, amid the poor dens of the earth,
> Quiet in a dark corner
> I sought in you, inflamed garland,
> My future dawns and furtive evening stars,
> And I glimpsed them in you,
> Natural and exact, also free and faithful,
> In my likeness,
> In your likeness, eternal solitude.

It shines into the "poor dens" as the light reflected into Plato's Cave to
give glimpses of man's deeper reality in time—"Natural and exact,
also free and faithful." As for the man, he lost that early fidelity to
himself: "Diverse with the world,/I was serene light and wild
eagerness,/And in the murky rain or the manifest sun/I wanted a
truth that would betray you." His error consisted in misunderstanding the true import of solitude and believing that it could be filled in
ordinary human terms through the company of man in his mere
semblance. Consequently, the veil of appearance dimmed his inner
light: "Forgetting in my anxiety/How fugitive wings create their own

cloud." The true vision of childhood was lost—"And . . . my eyes
became veiled/With clouds upon clouds of overflowing autumn"—in
exchange for transitory, hollow realities: "I denied you for very
little;/For trifling loves neither true nor false,/For quiet, seemly,
easy-chair friendships."

Although solitude has returned to the speaker, it does not bring
back to him his early self: "Because of you I now find myself the echo
of the erstwhile person/That I was." No longer the inner "inflamed
garland" but rather the beam of the lighthouse, still it brings solace—
"And you give me strength and weakness." But the vibrancy is gone;
the beam of the lighthouse offers but a resigned, cold repose like that
of stone: "As to the tired bird, the arms of the rock." The "fugitive
wings" have come to rest. The light is there, but it is a hard, external
one: "I am in the night a diamond that turns, warning men." The
speaker's love for man—"Their names now forgotten, I love them as
multitudes"—is equally lukewarm, impersonal.

A cosmic awareness is still possible in solitude: "You, solitary
truth,/Transparent passion, my solitude of always,/Are an immense
embrace;/The sun, the sea,/The darkness, the steppe." Possible also
is a vague love for undifferentiated humanity: "Because of you, my
solitude, I sought them once;/In you, my solitude, I love them now"
(*RD*, 106–8). But the contact with that true essence of man seen early
according to its inner light, its empathy with nature, has been lost.

While the pure vision of childhood is ultimately unattainable,
something may yet be salvaged from disparate appearance that can at
least regain for the poet some fragment of truth, and reaffirm his
belief in the harmony upholding the real. And the real, he tells us,
remains the poet's material, his bridge to that unity beyond: ". . .
only in the union of extremes can we intuit a harmony in the human
powers of comprehension. What do we know of what our life may be
in the thought of the gods? Everything is essential and necessary to
us, because in everything there vibrates an echo of poetry, and poetry
is nothing but the expression of that obscure daemonic force that
governs the world."[22] Cernuda came to read the pre-Socratics later,
while at Mount Holyoke, and was particularly struck by those
fragments attributed to Heraclitus. It is easy to see from the words
just quoted that already in 1936 his mind was curiously attuned to the
thoughts of the early Greek philosophers, and that his own poetic
investigation was parallel to their search for the underlying perma-
nence of the changing universe: "They do not comprehend how,
though it is at variance with itself, it agrees with itself. It is a harmony

of opposed tensions, as in the bow and the lyre,"[23] says Heraclitus. And Cernuda certainly believed the true poet to partake precisely of this understanding, of possessing some part of the "daemonic force." It allows him to find in nature that divine, elusive element of which love is the most immediate expression:

> But I listen; there resounds
> Through the thin air,
> A stellar melody,
> An echo amid the elms.
> I hear light caresses,
> I hear lighter kisses,
> Yonder wings beat,
> Yonder secrets pass.
>
> (*RD*, 108–10)[24]

"Por unos tulipanes amarillos" ("For Some Yellow Tulips") describes the fleeting visitation of a bearer of that tantalizing love revealing itself as both a human contact and a natural force: "For a fluttering from lip to lip/I sealed the pact, the sky and the earth were joined" (*RD*, 111–12).

Halfway through *Invocations* Cernuda encountered Hölderlin: "As I discovered, word by word, Hölderlin's text, the poetic depth and beauty of the same seemed to elevate me toward the highest that poetry can offer us" (*PL*, 194). His interest in myth, reinforced by this meeting with the German poet's work, acquired an importance far greater than that of a fertile ground for metaphor as another means of interpreting suprahuman reality. "Himno a la tristeza" ("Hymn to Sorrow"), written after Cernuda had read Hölderlin, reflects this backward look to the pagan world. In this poem sorrow plays a role reminiscent of that of solitude in "Soliloquy of the Lighthousekeeper"; but the emotion is seen in the guise of an ancient deity whose intercession is necessary to move toward cosmic awareness: ". . . you, celestial concealed bestower,/Never take your eyes from men/Your children, scourged by evil" (*RD*, 112–25). The last poem of the sequence, "A las estatuas de los dioses" ("To the Statues of the Gods"), is an even more explicit invocation of the pagan gods, an effort to bring back their past splendor, the image of ancient man's own glory: "Creatures, devoted and free, moved as water moves,/A reflection of your truth;/Glittering evil had not yet eaten away/Their bodies, full of majesty and grace." Our present condition is a lapse from heroic days: "Don't then judge sorry decadent humanity/With

lightning, war or plague." The poet's yearning for the state of grace is
an offering to the gods; only he and nature remember their glory:

> Meanwhile the poet, in the autumn night,
> Under the white lunatic ecstasy
> Gazes at the branches,
> Piously whitening themselves with light
> As their greenness abandons them;
> He dreams of your golden throne
> Of your blinding countenance,
> Far away from man,
> Out there in the impenetrable heavens.
>
> (PC, 46–49)

The beauty and light of Greek myth presented for Cernuda a
glaring contrast with what he saw as the sadness of traditional Roman
Catholic belief: "Why were you taught to bow your head before
deified suffering, when in another time men were so happy as to
adore beauty in its tragic plenitude?"[25] *Invocations* is his effort to
recapture the latent harmony of nature as it is expressed in myth,
through the creation of his own mythical imagery and the remolding
of that of ancient times. He sees in those early gods not only man's
awareness of the world's underlying harmony but also a source of his
own poetic intuition: "Whatever aspiration there is in you toward
poetry, it was those Hellenic myths that promoted and directed it."[26]

V *Conclusion*

The first moment of Cernuda's development from *First Poems* to
Invocations already contains in explicit or suggested form all the
principal constituents of his poetry, from broad concerns to
metaphorical characteristics. The sweeping oscillation that takes the
speaker in these compositions from a quasi-mystical yearning for the
world to its brooding rejection was evident in *First Poems*, remained
in *Where Oblivion Dwells* and *Invocations*, and will continue until
The Disconsolate Chimera. The world of man exhibits generally the
most alienating aspect of reality; that of nature, its most welcoming.
Certain components of this latter realm prove a particularly fruitful
source of imagery, and Cernuda will in fact retain his predilection for
them: the sea, light, and trees.

One basic ambiguity makes its appearance now and is to remain
unresolved: the poet is privileged to see because he has remained
close to nature as ordinary man has not, the latter losing his capacity

to understand and to love in proportion to his distance from the natural world; but the poet is only privileged to speak—to speak poetically, that is—insofar as he is a sophisticated artificer, a creator of form. This apparent contradiction is born of Cernuda's concept of poetic vision as the near revelation of an ideal reality whose re-creation can be but approximate. His solution is that beauty and love are expressions of that ideal and that the poem may in its turn express them. In this sense, the artificial participates in the essential. Man's creations can sometimes protect the natural, even create propitious circumstances for its flourishing. Thus, the "hidden garden" is comparable to the poem in that they both constitute artificial organizations of beauty whereby the poet may meet with or give form to his deepest yearnings. The desired mystical union is as infrequent as it is insistently sought and consists as much in the intuitive understanding of nature's inner harmony as in the actual communion with it.

These early works represent for Cernuda a period of necessary investigation on various fronts. From the point of view of his craft, *First Poems* and *Eclogue, Elegy, Ode* demonstrated his natural ease with classical forms while exhausting their interest for him. With respect to his inner self, *A River, A Love* and *Forbidden Pleasures* allowed him the freedom to speak out and to explore those aspects of himself heretofore hidden for the sake of social convention. *Where Oblivion Dwells* reflects the underlying duality of his work, in the investigation of the moment of recoil from the world and in the discovery of a possible merging, though dark and joyless, as the annihilating plunge into oblivion. *Invocations*, on the other hand, explores facets of intuition, or means of obtaining insights from reality or from oneself, as stages in the search for the illuminating conjunction with nature.

CHAPTER 3

The Clouds: *The Exile in Time*

I *Introduction*

A S we look back upon Cernuda's work so far, there arises a broad rhythm of composition, wherein a period of strong reaction to circumstance is followed by one of resignation or even, infrequently, of hope. In the first instance, his poetry may range from invective to despair, in the second, from quiet skepticism to serenity. After the anger of *A River, A Love,* came the calmer mood of *Forbidden Pleasures;* likewise, the somberness of *Where Oblivion Dwells* was mitigated by the hopeful seeking of *Invocations.* Such is again the case with the two collections examined in this chapter and the one to follow. In *Las Nubes (The Clouds)* Cernuda views the world with a bitter, critical eye—there are perhaps three or four exceptions out of the thirty-one poems comprising the collection—while in *Como quien espera el alba (Like Someone Waiting for the Dawn)* a more tranquil tone prevails.

Principal still among Cernuda's themes are time and its corollary ideas: death, the supreme evidence of man's temporality; memory, a generally insufficient ally; desire, or love, both the means to arrest decay and at the same time the most painful reminder of its inevitability. The presence of Spain is significant in the *The Clouds,* when the Civil War was still raging or had just ended, but will diminish in *Like Someone Waiting for the Dawn,* to be replaced by the more impersonal nostalgia of exile from the home, the poet's condition on earth. Cernuda's pantheistic assertions of *Invocations* acquire, on occasion, more specifically Christian overtones, although his attitude toward organized religion remains on the whole negative. He is never to lose his distaste for the elements of fear and sadness which he detects in Christianity, albeit his frequent yearnings for the innocence of childhood may include nostalgia for its beliefs. In general, his God is

50

more pagan than it is Christian, akin to some sort of harmonizing cosmic force quite untouched by dogma.

From the point of view of form, it is in this stage of his work that Cernuda achieves his mature manner. He makes more frequent use of the dramatic monologue—we saw an early instance of it in "Soliloquy of the Lighthousekeeper"—and at times resorts to the second-person form of address, the speaker in the poems communicating with his other self as "tú." The poems, if frequently long, are tighter in structure, the language more straightforward, generally rid of the rhetoricism which burdened some of his work up through *Invocations*.

The Clouds first appeared in the second edition of *Reality and Desire*, published under the editorship of José Bergamín in Mexico City in 1940. The poems in this book were begun in Spain in 1937 and completed in England in 1940. The period of their composition was probably the most turbulent in Cernuda's life: the Civil War had broken out, he traveled to France, returned to Spain, and finally established himself in England under less than ideal conditions. In the damp English countryside first and then in the cold of Scotland, exile, for a son of bright Andalusia, was all the more bitter and forbidding. This was particularly so in the case of a poet like Cernuda, so sensitive to his environment that the quality of sunlight, for instance, could constitute a first step toward the longed-for concord with nature.[1]

It is then not surprising to find that the majority of the poems in *The Clouds* express a decidedly pessimistic vision; the world is chaotic, history moves through bloodshed toward emptiness. Our life is, to use Heidegger's phrase—whose more negative implications Cernuda would probably have subscribed to at this time—"being toward death." In his empty gesticulating, man can neither resist nor avoid the undertow of time. A misunderstanding of its forces leads him to emphasize and submit to that which is most ephemeral: the evidence of power, the illusion of control over his destiny, passing affections.

II *The Fall into History*

"Noche de luna ("Moonlit Night"), the first poem of this group, is characteristic in its negative view of history as a decline toward nothingness. A contrast between the moon's impassive gaze and the turbulence of human events is established from the first stanza and initiated as a life-virginity opposition: "Life after life, men/Went on forgetting/That virgin goddess." In contrast to "that virgin goddess," "life after life" already acquires slight fertility—that is, erotic—connotations; in the second stanza the equation of human struggle and Eros becomes clearer: ". . . agile and naked they take possession/Of this earth, with tremulous dominion,/As the lover/ Seizes and penetrates the loved body." The race whose history is being described is now still climbing vigorously toward its peak, impetuous rather than brutal. An equilibrium is reached in stanza three. Eros manifests itself in terms of its social significance, another element in the process of establishment and expansion: "Later, she [the moon] saw their works, their cohabitations." The fourth and fifth stanzas present the race at its apex, but this culminating finds its expression in war and enslavement:

> She looked upon their long wars
> With enemy peoples
> And the sacred scourge
> Of fratricidal struggles;
> . . . .
> She also looked upon the plough
> Passing with the serf
> Over the ancient battlefield,
> Fertilized by so many young bodies;
> And upon that same ground she later saw running
> The prideful owner on stout horses,
> While the grass, nettle and thistle
> Grew over the vast estates.

Images of sterility prevail in these last lines; young blood first fertilized the land, but once won, the fields were left fallow. Time begins to assert its grasp: there is now a history—"the ancient battlefield"—established by war. This fifth stanza also contains the broadest temporal span—"she looked," "has later seen running," "were growing"—the increased activity of time is equated with the increased importance of death.

Eros, which had earlier retained its connotations of fecundity now spends itself futilely; it is but another aspect of death: "How much virile semen/She saw surging amid spasms/Of bodies today undone/In the wind and the dust." Death and waste reign as time passes ever more quickly: "How many clear ruins/Barely adorned with mustard plants/Did she once see as strong castles." The fertile women of previous stanzas appear now cold and remote, finding pleasure also in death—the hunt—their love no longer fruitful:

> Stones more eloquent than the centuries,
> Trod upon before by the light step
> Of svelte huntresses, a falcon on their fist,
> Their sleepy gaze aslant
> Between boredom and a clandestine love.

In stanza eight the moon's presence takes on its more deadly aspect: "It pours, bluish urn,/Its lethal enchantment." Man has spent himself. Before the final disappearance, it is the poet's turn. His dream may abstract deeds from time and give them a measure of eternity:

> And the Magical reflection amid the trees
> Allows the dreamer to surrender to song,
> To pleasure and to rest,
> To what being ephemeral is dreamed as eternal.

History has been written. It will but repeat itself in continuing cycles of death until the virgin goddess sees in the earth a reflection of herself: "The silence of a world that has been/And the pure beauty of nothingness" (*RD*, 129–31). The goddess has remained distant throughout although some slight modifications occur within this aloofness. In the first stanza she attends with "peaceful love." At this time man is still in the process of forgetting, and tenuous links remain between him and his deity. In stanzas two to seven she is content to look—the only verbs used are "she saw" several times, "she contemplated" once, and "she looked" twice—but from stanza eight on, she begins to exert some effect upon the earth: "It pours. . ."; "her reflection/divulges the presence of the sea"; and her reflection is instrumental in the poet's dream (stanza nine). This moment signals the peak of her activity. In the last stanza the goddess is once more a mere gaze.

The implication of a "fault" or sin on the part of man, the forgetting of an original condition, weighs heavily on the poem. The moon, as an image of the mother goddess, possesses the two basic potentialities of the archetype: great mother and great destroyer.[2] Here Cernuda chooses to intimate her power as the great destroyer. This possibility seems an aspect of her calm contemplation so that it is man himself who bears the burden of self-destruction. Although fallen, early man retains the potential of youth; erotic vigor appears as yet fruitful, though not entirely free from its darker aspects. Soon it becomes wholly a thirst for power and leads to war. It spends itself ultimately in sterile fevers.

According to Derek Harris[3] this poem was originally titled "Elegía a la luna de España" ("Elegy to the Moon of Spain"). There is little in the poem actually allowing one to conclude that Spain is particularly intended as the "ancient/Dwelling of men"; rather, the earth as a whole seems more likely intended in the final "silence of a world that has been." The poem in any case transcends specific geographical location to acquire broader significance as a vision of man's struggle "unto death", of which Cernuda's wartime Spain was a tragic instance. This composition contains several important ideas explored by Cernuda in *The Clouds:* man's temporal condition as a creature living with death; love and death as twin, ultimately interchangeable forces; the role of the poet as one whose energies are directed toward transcending temporality; Spain, perhaps by implication here, as a striking, painful instance of self-destruction. Prevalent among these preoccupations is a concern with time. It plays some role in almost all the poems of the collection and is also in a considerable number of them the principal subject of meditation. Not infrequently, several of these recurring motifs are concentrated in single poems as facets of a central concern with the futility of man's undertakings under the pall of death.

III   *"Against All Death's Endeavour"*[4]

"A un poeta muerto (F. G. L.)" ("To a Dead Poet [F. G. L.]"), the second poem of *The Clouds,* examines the problem of the poet's worth in his land (Spain), his role in general, and seeks to know whether any meaning may be discovered in the poet's death through the example of Lorca. Lorca's premature and violent death, as well as its peculiar senselessness in the midst of the broader insanity of the Civil War, makes the instance particularly striking. The basic duality that the poem is to pursue appears in the first lines:

> As on the rock we never see
> The light flower opening,
> Among a people sullen and hard
> The fresh and tall adornment of life
> Does not beautifully shine.
> That is why they killed you, because you were
> Greenness in our arid land
> And blue in our dark air.

Against the aridity of the land rises the fresh and fertile openness of the poet: light against darkness, color against grayness. The poem then pursues this initial opposition; the lighter, more insubstantial reality that the poet seems to represent when contrasted with the impervious hostility in man's heart acquires weight through being an expression of even deeper energies: "But an immense hidden yearning warns/That its unknown spur may only/Be placated within us with death." Finally, these forces are indentified with the deity:

> Because this divine longing, lost here on earth
> After so much pain and abandonment,
> With its own greatness advises us
> Of some immense creating mind,
> That conceives the poet as the tongue of its glory
> And then consoles him beyond death.

What happened to Lorca in Spain is only an acute example, in times of crisis, of what befalls all poets on earth. For it is in the nature of the poet to seek that ultimate union transcending appearance which only death allows: "For the poet death is the victory."

A similar light falls on the poet in "A Larra con unas violetas" ("To Larra with a Few Violets"); he is a stranger on man's earth: "There is no room in it for the lone man/Naked and dazzling son of the divine thought." And, as in comparison to Lorca's memory, "These men are shadows", so is this world but "another silence where fear commands." In this poem also Cernuda speaks clearly as a poet taking his stand with Larra, alienated from the society of men:

> He who already speaks to the dead,
> Is found mute by those who live,
> And in this other silence, where fear commands,
> To gather the flowers, one by one
> Was a brief consolation amid the days
> Whose bloody footprint is borne on shoulders
> Laden by hate with a useless stone.

The contrast between the burden borne by the living poet's time— "bloody footprint," "useless stone"—and the tribute placed on the tomb—"A few violets,/. . . /Fresh amid the fog"—suggests a yearning for the peace of death in the speaker similar to that which must have led Larra to suicide. The writer in Spain is a dead man walking,

unheard and unheeded. In Larra, the negation of speech is equated
with the negation of life:

> To write in Spain is not to cry, but to die,
> Because inspiration dies wrapped in smoke,
> When its flame does not go free after the wind.
> Thus, when love, the tender blond monster,
> Turned against you so many vain endearments,
> Your hand opened death, red and vast, with a gunshot.

The suicide transcends its limited condition of protest against love
denied to become a protest against poetry denied; and we know that
for Cernuda love and poetry are both moments of the same essential,
vital struggle against temporality. Larra's work finds its echo in the
words of the twentieth-century poet. It is both his and Cernuda's
consolation that, although "The word is brief as the bird's song," brief
as the romantic writer's life, and light also as the offered flowers, it
may not altogether be dampened "wrapped in smoke" but rather
"climb, sentinel angel, who bears witness to man,/There up to the
celestial and impassive region" (*RD*, 140–42).

Cernuda's most frequent determination of death places it within us
and around us, a presence as inescapable as that of time. "Cementerio
en la ciudad" ("Urban Cemetery"), one of the best poems in *The
Clouds,* develops in a correlative sequence the image of an urban
cemetery as a city of the dead within a city of the living dead. This
poem has been generally viewed as a censure of man's indifference
toward the dead. While such an interpretation is essentially correct,
it represents perhaps too partial a view of the poem. The piece's true
import becomes clearer with the shift of emphasis that another
possible reading of the last line suggests: "Acaso Dios también se
olvida de vosotros." E. M. Wilson translates it as "Perhaps God also
has forgotten you."[5] One can see that reading it as "Perhaps God has
forgotten you also" transforms the overtones of the poem while
maintaining Cernuda's reference to God in a perspective that is, for
him, more customary. In effect, it clearly situates dead and living on
the same plane within God's indifference. Contrary to Alexander
Coleman's statement that ". . . the materialism that the city embodies for Cernuda has afforded him an appropriate focus for an
atheistic vision of life,"[6] it is not a strict atheism that Cernuda
professes; rather it is the refusal—and not consistently at that—to
believe in a personal God at all involved with mankind and his
preference for a sort of cosmic unity or force devoid of prescriptive

content. Precisely one of the elements of the agony of the dead and the dejection of the living is their decision to place their faith in a nonexistent or forgetful God.

Beyond this, seeing the dead and the living from the same point of view allows a series of parallelisms to emerge in the poem that reinforce the central one: city = cemetery. The first lines of the second stanza appear as correlative statements equating tombstones and housefronts: "Cloths damp with rain hang from the windows/ Like patches on the gray housefronts./The Epitaphs are obliterated/ On the tombstones of two centuries of dead." Preceding these lines in stanza one we read ". . . wooden benches, where /Old People sit in silence of an evening" and following them in stanza two: ". . . But when the sun wakes/(For the sun shines on a few days about June)/Their old bones must feel something below there." Furthermore, the objective descriptions of the cemetery are applicable to the city as a whole: ". . . between walls black earth/—No trees or grass—." Stanza three, in its entirety, refers equally to the city and the cemetery:

> Not a leaf, not a bird. Stone, nothing else.
>   and earth.
> Is Hell like this? Here is grief without
>   forgetfulness
> With noise and poverty, long hopeless cold.
> Here is no silent sleep of death, for life
> Yet moves among these graves, just as a prostitute
> Continues business under the still night.

Life moves thus among the tomblike housefronts as well as among the tombstones, spurious as a prostitute's affection. The awakened bodies of the last lines are no more dead than the city's dwellers:

> When the shadow falls from the clouded sky
> And the factory smoke has dwindled to gray dust,
> Shouts come from the public house, a passing train
> Shakes the long echoes like an angry bugle.
> It is not the Jugment yet; you nameless dead
> Keep still and sleep; sleep, if you can sleep.
> Perhaps God has forgotten you also. [7]

(*PC*, 65)

Signs of life have "dwindled to gray dust," while the dead must be enjoined to "Keep still and sleep." In this dark mood Cernuda sees no more consolation in death than he finds fulfillment in a life shackled by duration.

IV   *The God's Appearance*

Cernuda's attitude toward nature, or reality, and toward death are but aspects of his intense awareness of time passing. Coupled with this awareness is the belief that temporality may be transcended, that it is transcended by certain forms of beauty, perhaps by true poetry. For there also remain two convictions: the first and most basic one which we have met already and shall encounter throughout shows a supreme unity subsisting behind apparent dispersion; the second, its corollary, is that the essential aspects of reality are not lost, that they return, for they are expressions of that lasting unity. To perceive and redeem such forms is to overcome death.

Yet Cernuda's struggle with time in *The Clouds* seldom results in such conquests. It is an uncertain battle, where the enemy is ever elusive and victories, should there be any, belong to the future. In "La visita de Dios" ("God's Visit") the poet wonders whether he has time left:

> Can I wait perhaps? All has been given to man
> As an ephemeral distraction from existence;
> He can join to nothing this, his yearning
>   that demands
> A pause of love amid the flight of things.

Time has been elevated to a divine plane, but it is an all-devouring divinity whose very existence depends on the sacrifice of life:

> Time, that white limitless desert,
> That creating nothingness, menaces men
> And opens with immortal light before youthful desires.
> Some want madly to seize its magical reflection,
> But others conjure it with a son
> Offered in arms as a victim,
> Because its life maintains itself with new life
> As water does with the water wept by men.

This stanza, while suggesting the Christian idea of God through that of the sacrificed son, alters it in such a manner that God becomes but another incarnation of the great pagan deity in need of propitiation.

The lines that follow make this meaning clear: "But you, God, with what shall we placate you?/You were my thirst, you were my love lost,/My broken home, my labored life . . ." (*RD*, 147–49). The God born within man, within the poet, is one of the facets of time, eliciting love and beauty in the shadow of its own menace. The redemption of man from time, the main function of the deity for Cernuda, remains invariably unconsummated because of the chasm separating humanity from the divine. "Undertow in Sansueña," for instance, acquires broader significance when read as a dramatic meditation on this distance. The composition, bearing the subtitle "Fragments of a Dramatic Poem," is divided into three parts: a "Prologue," seemingly the objective description of early day in a southern setting; the "Monologue of the Statue," where the statue of a fallen god muses on its fate; and a "Conclusion" describing the land and its inhabitants at nightfall.

The Mediterranean sunrise of the "Prologue," echoing Homer's rosy-fingered dawn, recalls an Andalusia in classical garb:

> It is the light dawn of summer
> In the Southern coast, when afar, an airy
> Suggestion of the light, rippling with pink
> Opens the mother of pearl of its sea and its sky.

As in the traditional prelude to a drama, the Edenic situation has only the appearance of tranquillity:

> But a blind statue gave to the people the legend
> Of some malignant power, lying in wait
> Since remote centuries in a drowned marble.
> Now begins the drama. Listen silently.

The stress on the dramatic elements of what is to follow enjoins the audience, the reader, to pay attention to the *exemplum*, the lesson to be learned from the story, while reminding him that there *is* a drama going on. The statue's story proceeds initially in terms of a then/now opposition: past glory, present darkness—"I am the divine stone/ Dashed by disaster from temple to abyss,/ . . ./I am the one adored by remote ages/As the form of the day. . . ." The god's defeat has signaled a submission to time and memory—"I am full of memories . . ."—and the continuing anticipation of future release: "I still await redemption from the deep waters." The section's last line, "Mortal form of a god defenseless among men," contradicts the warning

issued at the end of the prologue—"Of some malignant power"—
implying that the hidden tragedy is that of the separation of a people
from their god and of confidence replaced by fear. Although this
tragedy appears to be that of the defeated god more than of the
apparently innocent and oblivious race, the former's fate cannot but
reverberate upon the latter. In the superficial calm of the "Conclusion", man is alone: "No voice answers man's pain/. . ./Over the
sleeping field, the slow night turns" (RD, 150–53). The drama resides
in the unawareness of our state, and the rhetoric of the poem which
announces that something is happening contrary to appearance is an
accurate reflection of that very unawareness.

The most specifically Christian of the poems in *The Clouds* is "La
adoraciòn de los Magos" ("The Adoration of the Magi"), though it is
more so in its subject than in its import.[8] The poem is in five parts. In
Part I, "The Eve," Melchior, oldest of the Magi, disillusioned with
life, expresses his desire for ultimate peace; upon seeing the star, sign
of God's coming, his hope to see the new God before he dies is
reawakened and he sets out. In Part II, "The Kings," the three Magi
reveal their conflicting desires; Gaspar and Balthasar see little point
in the search to which Melchior constrains them; the threat of
violence upon their lands by Melchior's armies—they are his
tributaries—persuades them to continue. Part III, "Palinode of
Divine Hope," reveals in a voice common to all three the kings'
disappointment upon finding an infant rather than God. In Part IV,
"On Time Past," a shepherd recounts the passing through the land of
that unusual procession of the three wise men, gold and silver shining
in the dust, and their eventual fate. Part V is an epitaph to the three
kings.

In Melchior's opening monologue the two principal elements are
time, undermining desire, and hope for desire's magical resurgence:
"Can the magic/Still be possible when youth and desire/Are
past? . . ." This desire, although expressed in sensuous terms, is the
need of the intellect for certainty, the wish for a measure of control
over time through the satisfaction of seeing therein a recognizable
pattern:

> Lord, grant us the peace of desire
> Satisfied, of life fulfilled,
> To be as the flower which grows and blooms,
> Breathing in peace, singing beneath
> The sunlit sky, even though death exists:
> The summit will melt into the slopes.

The Lord answers not, however, but the Devil: "Glory to God in the highest, / Earth over men in their hell." Here is already summarized the perennial rift between man and the God he invents through his invocation. There is to be no response from God, no recognition from the king. As the leader of the pilgrimage, his failure here anticipated will be that of all three. This failure is further intimated in the appearance of the star whose light Melchior sees "flowing / Joyously like blood from a wound," an echo of its earlier description "Like a tear on an Ethiopian cheek." Both images announce the future defeat of Jesus through man's—and the Magi's—rejection of his divinity.

In Part II the three kings reveal the true meaning of their quest and the reason for its frustration. It is not God who creates man in his own image, but man who creates God after himself. What Melchior interprets as Gaspar's and Balthasar's willful refusal to understand his truth leads him to threaten them with force, and his apparently spiritual search reveals itself as a striving for power, the trajectory of all traditional human faith:

> Melchior: Madmen enamoured of shadows, do you forget that your king-
> doms
> Are subject to me, that I can still force you to follow
> The track of my star, among the barefoot slaves?
> What is pride or pleasure beside the fear, the great sin, the force
> of the earth?
> Balthasar: With your truth, if we find it, we might raise a great empire.
> Gaspar: Perhaps, like the Spring, that truth will unveil crimson desires.

While their purposes are superficially different, the kings' impulse is the same; they want a truth that will allow them to re-create reality according to their individual desires. Having found this impossible heretofore, they were willing to submit to the power of a God who would undertake such a task for them. But their view of this God continues as individual as their view of reality and is similarly limited: Jesus remains a weak, human infant; not responding to any of the ideas of truth held by the three Magi, he is a God in none of their worlds: "We had hoped for a god, / . . ./ We found a life like our human life, / . . ./ A harvest for death to reap."

Part IV, "On Time Past," consists in an anonymous shepherd's tale of those past events now distant in time. The initial stanzas set the tale against the background of the earth's cyclical fecundity and the shepherd's unvarying tasks:

> Look how the yellow light of evening
> Spreads its long embrace over the earth
> On the hillside, gliding the autumn-gray
> Of olives heavy now with ripe fruit.
>
> Look there at the mist shining on the swamp.
> Here, year after year, our life goes by,
> By day we take the flocks across the plain
> Beside the brackish water's grassy banks;

Within the changeless rhythms of time, man's endeavors—those of
kings as well as those of shepherds—seem inconsequential. The
shepherd's closeness to nature and his unquestioning acceptance of
its inevitable transformations allow him to see the Magi's inquiry with
little sympathy and yet with greater clarity: "They were kings made
mad by power and leisure." They saw "Man's poverty, which before
they had not known," a truth too small to meet their yearning. But in
the search for greater certainties, they lost the smaller ones that they
possessed:

> People in the market spoke of the Kings:
> One died on the journey, far from his land;
> Another lost his throne, made beggar or slave;
> Another lived alone, a prey to sadness.

Even in the case of Melchior, whose fate appears less drastic, the loss
was equally decisive, since he no longer had the hope of the magical
prophecy to fill his loneliness.

The shepherd's concluding remarks are revealing in the light of
Christian tradition:

> They sought a new god, and some say they found him.
> I rarely saw men. I have never seen any gods.
> How can an ignorant shepherd see gods?
> Look over there at the blood-red setting sun.
>
> (PC, 68–85)

The new god did not reveal himself to the shepherds either: "Suns
and moons passed. I was young. I am old." They were untouched by
his coming, but then they had not called for or expected him. The sun
seems the only evidence of divinity, seen here in terms of its
self-sacrifice, but also as the unaffected evidence of time. And that has
not changed. The kings' separation from the god, their unquenched

thirst for eternity, is not as cruel a fate as the gods' own distance from man. Death, states the Epitaph (Part V) is the end of all yearning: "Now death lulls their desires, / Sated at last. . . ." The severance insinuated by the Devil in Part I in response to Melchior's prayer has not been joined. The truth that they found—"They sought the truth, and found it, / But did not believe"—was not the one to echo their desire, but rather that of man's misery, known also to the shepherd, trivial and yet massive in its denial of their hoped-for deity.

In this poem Cernuda expresses the full vigor of the struggle between reality and desire, the anguish of unattainable belief. Only the voice of the shepherd suggests a possible solution in a life of harmony but whose limited scope is as difficult to comply with as metaphysical desire is to fulfill. From the point of view of form, Cernuda's use of dramatized voices reaches here its full potential, enabling him to explore and contrast conflicting aspects of his own self, while not allowing the projected voice any loss of intensity.

The distance between man and his gods is identical with that between man's imagination and the visible world, or in the poet's terms, between desire and reality. Cernuda's vision of the divine is linked with his struggle against the destructive flow of time in that it represents the certainty of the unchanging, but the deity must by definition remain separate, unattainable by our living selves. For Cernuda it is an unresolvable paradox that the union with God should be ours only after death, since our need for him belongs to our life and exists only as a refusal of death. The Christian God whom man has exalted, and who has manifested Himself through His own death among us, has reserved eternity for Himself and does not generally answer Cernuda's pressing need to fulfill and broaden his living present.

Among the poems of *Ocnos*, written for the most part during the years of exile in England as was *The Clouds*, "La nieve" ("The Snow") evidences this rejection of the Christian myth in precisely such terms: "A homely memory attributes enchantment to it, [snow] when father, mother, progeny, like an illuminated print, exchange smiles and gifts before a dead pine, as before an altar, while outside in wait snow surrounds them; this same cruel snow, sterile, irrevocable. There you have one, and not the least of the inconsistencies customary to the common mind: to find as the myth of life that one where life precisely does not exist, unless there is expressed with it an unconscious desire of annihilation in the paschal summit of human triviality (*O*, 157–58).

V *God and the Living*

And yet God need not be as insufficient as man has made him. We have cut him to the size of our smallness and our fear. Cernuda calls for a God vaster and yet closer to us, one in whose divinity we participate as fragments of eternity, the God that time hides from us. Some poems of *The Clouds* are meditations on the relationship possible with a God who does not call for the denial of life or its despising. These poems are best read as inquiries on possible manifestations of the divine, born of an unvarying yearning for completeness, in which a higher harmony becomes perceptible through external signs.

At times, the expectation of a fuller future is manifested in reflections that approximate, though they do not meet with, traditional religion. In *The Clouds* "Cordura" ("Sound Judgment") constitutes one of Cernuda's calmer considerations of man's postlapsarian condition in the light of self-serving belief. The ideal state hinted at in this poem existed in the past and is expected again; life, for the exiled poet, is a remembrance and an anticipation:[9] "A deep feeling/Of past joys/Turned to oblivion beneath/The earth, fills the afternoon." The poet cannot reach other souls, men are around him as mere physical presences. The God he knows offered no Son on the cross. There was no intermediary, no punishment, no redemption. There has been a forgetting: "It is hard to find oneself alone/In the midst of bodies./But his love has that form:/The cross with no one." God's love is to be a direct illumination which the poet awaits. Upon that new day communion will be possible with his "fellowmen," no longer mere bodies: "Because of that love I hope,/Awake in his lap/To find on a pure dawn/Communion with men" (*RD*, 155–57).

The expectation of a luminous future where man may find unity in a God not merely Christian gives way in "Atardecer en la catedral" ("Evening in the Cathedral") to an apparently contradictory impulse, where the speaker seeks the solace of traditional religion in the cathedral, epitome of centuries-old Catholic aspirations. However, it is the value of the building as a symbol of the accumulated desire of man for God and as a haven of repose that is stressed, irrespective of dogmatic differentiation. Insofar as it expresses God's existence, adumbrating the mystery of divinity, the cathedral retains its power:

> Scents, live sproutings surge,
> Affirming life, as a sap of the earth
> That breaks through in miraculous green forms,

> Secret between the walls of this temple,
> The animating breath of our world
> Passes by and refreshes the night of man.
>
> (*RD*, 153–55)

There is throughout the poem a clear avoidance of specific religious connotation, most clearly so in this last stanza, and an emphasis on the building's power to bring peace. Such indeterminacy of doctrinal content allows the cathedral to transcend its temporal and ritual limitations, to acquire greater significance in the immemorial genealogy of great structures devoted to the concept of deity.

In the great poem "Lázaro" ("Lazarus") based on the Gospel story Cernuda expounds, through one of his most successful projected voices, both the acceptance of a melancholy life in exile and the hope of eventual spiritual renewal. He looks back to its composition with unaccustomed satisfaction: " 'Lazarus,' one of my favorite compositions, wanted to express that disenchanted surprise, as if, after dying, I were to return again to life"(*PL*, 200). If is significant that there should be no mention of Christ as such throughout the entire poem. Lazarus refers to him as one would to a man of unusual abilities, filled with great compassion and power in love: "Then deep below the forehead I saw the eyes/Full of compassion, trembling I found a soul/In which my soul was infinitely copied/By love, mistress of the world." Lazarus' return to life is more a rebirth to suffering than a reawakening, a call to bow once more under a burden he had hoped to cast off forever: "Again I felt the dream,/The madness and mistake of being alive/When we are flesh that suffers day by day." His resurrection is described as the penetration of cold and pain into a blissfully quiescent body: "I can remember nothing but a strange cold/ . . ./—Eager to be transformed to lukewarm blood—." His new life is a continuation of forgotten death: "Only broad cerements, yellow strips of linen,/Heavy in smell, laid bare/Gray flesh, soft like a sleepy fruit;/Not the smooth dark body, rose of the desires,/But the body of a son of death." The body has arisen, but the spirit—"rose of the desires"—has not been called forth. Lazarus' initial impulse is to find again the oblivion of death. In strikingly powerful imagery, he recalls his soul's tortured, anguished recalcitrance:

> I tried to close my eyes, to seek
> The vast shadow, the primal darkness
> That hides its sources underneath the world
> And washes memory free of shame.

> When an aching soul inside my bowels
> Sent through the dark galleries of my body
> A bitter, jangling shriek
> Until it struck against the wall of bone
> And raised the tides of fever in my blood.

The soul is now once more trapped—"the wall of bone"—shackled to mortal matter. Lazarus' first physical movements in his new life are the reflection of those earlier ones toward death, making of the latter a deliverance, of the former an enslavement: ". . . I went in silence/ Though it was all empty and strange for me, /And I was thinking: 'So must they have walked, /So carried me to the earth when I was dead.' "

For Lazarus, Christ's action is a summons to renewed penitence. But he sees in his eyes the reflection of God's truth, if not God. And he understands that God transcends the limitations of need as he does those of his creation. He does not ask help of Jesus as God, but of God through this compassionate man, Jesus:

> His hand lay near, I leant my head upon it,
> Loathing my body and my soul.
> . . . .
> So did I ask with tears for
> Strength to bear my ignorance with resignation,
> To work neither for my life nor for my spirit
> But for a truth I had half seen in those eyes
> Then. Beauty is patience. I
> Know that the lily of the field
> After its humble darkness night after night,
> Its long waiting under ground, from
> Its straight green stalk to its white crown of petals,
> Will one day blossom in triumphant glory.[10]

The final metaphor pictures Lazarus' new life as another burial, one from which he hopes to rise to the light of truth, when he participates in the divine spirit. Delivered from time once, Lazarus finds that again he must submit to it. From the beginning the resurrection had appeared as a return to temporality: "It was early morning. /. . . they had worked hard to lift the stone, /For time, not matter, weighed it down." The paradox of life-as-death makes of the nascent daylight a threat and of the night ending a tempting restfulness. The initial lines of almost all the early stanzas refer to a growing light seen in terms of death, or, as contradictory to our usual connotations of life:

> Someone spoke of a new birth
> But there was no mother's blood . . .
> . . . .
> The air was calm, but the bodies trembled—
> . . . .
> The man who held the lantern,
> The witness of the miracle,
> Roughly put out the flame.—
>
> (PC, 52–59)

An interesting extrapolation suggests itself here in a comparison of the light and darkness images. For light appears in its limiting aspect, as daytime, but darkness is "The vast shadow, the primal darkness." Lazarus's wish to return to darkness is then conceivable as a wish to be reintegrated within the pretemporal earth mother.[11] Since this is denied him, he wants to grow into the eternal, supratemporal light, out of the earth and beyond its surface, so to speak, beyond its time-bound character (". . . white crown of petals, / Will one day blossom in triumphant glory"). Thus Lazarus's true resurrection is the one he awaits beyond his present life. It contrasts with the earth's darkness (". . . humble darkness night after night") as whiteness and true light, the fully differentiated spirit that sees "a truth . . . half seen."

VI   *"Beauty Past Change"*[12]

"El ruiseñor sobre la piedra" ("The Nightingale on the Stone"), last poem of *The Clouds,* is chronologically the first one[13] of those linked to the figure of Philip II, although it concerns more specifically the Escorial and not its kingly builder. It stands in marked contrast to those earlier poems of this collection expressing a bitter, negative view of Spain in that the palace-monastery emerges as the epitome of the country's spirit and yet is an image of beauty in Cernuda's northern exile. Also, in this composition Cernuda is moving into a period of calmer contemplation, penetrated by more frequent glimmers of hope. In such moments the perennial values of beauty reaffirm themselves as those aspects of man's creation participating in the eternal, and his own potential victory over flux.

The poem is the poet's mental re-creation of the monastery as well as a meditation on his exile and on what the edifice means to him:

> A serene lily erected on stone
> You seem, near the monastery's orchard

> A bright nightingale amid the pines
> Raised by a silent song.
> Or the fruit of the pomegranate, rough on the outside,
> But promising and juicy in what is hidden.
> Thus, Escorial, does my memory see you.
> If you rise hard to the broad skies,
> On the serene water of the pond
> Turned graceful, you smile. And the clouds
> Crown your immortal designs.

At the heart of this first stanza stands the poet and his vision: "Thus, Escorial, does my memory see you." This line contains the three principal elements of the poem: (1) the monastery (Escorial); (2) the poet's activity ("see you"); (3) the source of that activity ("my memory"). The monastery is a rising architecture of whiteness, a song— the poet's effusion—and a structure of hidden beauty—the poem. The body of the composition elaborates each one of these themes in threefold interdependence until an indissoluble relationship is created between the poet and his role as creator and the Escorial as the epitome of Spain, itself creating the country's spirit as it embodies it. The final strophe is:

> Thus do I sing you now, because you are
> Cheerful, with the tragic titanic joy
> Of stones, that binds harmony
> Tying it to the choir of mountains.
> Because you are our very life,
> But not one perishable,
> Rather eternal, with its stubborn longings
> Attained for ever and ever new
> Under a shadowless light.
> And if your image trembles in the extended waters,
> It is merely an image;
> And if time takes us, drowning so much unsatisfied
>   yearning,
> It is only as a dream;
> For your will of stone is to live,
> It is to live, and us with you.

(RD, 179–82)

The final strophe is the poet's own direct affirmation of his task, the conclusion to this reordering of the monastery's architecture into a structure of words. The first lines, whose powerful stresses call forth the classical *lira* Strophe, are like the blocks of granite of the building. Previous ideas correlated with the Escorial are recapitulated now in coda fashion with the full wake of references that they have gathered. The poet's song, for instance—"Thus do I sing you now . . ."—is also that of the monastery's builders, lovers of beauty; his own song as an exile, a mere man; that of the people of Spain in general, those who were truly their country's children; the frozen harmony that the building itself is; the nightingale's gratuitous paean; the poem itself. The central part of the strophe rises on the stately foundation of the first four lines as a hymn to a life's yearning for eternity. Once the Escorial has become an element of eternity in the life of the exile and his embattled countrymen alike, present and personal distresses are but ripples on the building's reflection: "And if your image trembles in the extended water, / It is merely an image"—compare with stanza one "On the serene water . . ./. . . you smile . . ."; the individual's subjection to time is less real than his own reflection drowned in a dream. As the plastic form of our desire, of Spain's spirit and dream of beauty, it lasts: " . . . your will of stone is to live / It is to live, and us with you."

Last poem of *The Clouds*, "The Nightingale on the Stone" asserts Cernuda's renewed confidence in the power of poetry to transcend the ephemeral nature of its maker; in like manner the Escorial transcends and epitomizes the will of its builders and of its age. As the image or, to use his own language, the sculptured form of the spirit of Spain, it remains unchanging, while history seems a mere concatenation of accidents incidental to its essence. In this poem Cernuda reaches the spare strength and clarity of his best works; a meditation, it is also a lyrical celebration approximating the purity of song which he felt was the attribute of all great poetry. In its serenity the composition already moves toward the pensive calm of *Like Someone Waiting for the Dawn*.

CHAPTER 4

Like Someone Waiting for the Dawn: *The Gaze Within*

I *Introduction*

*C*omo quien espera el alba *(Like Someone Waiting for the Dawn)*
was included in the 1958 edition of *Reality and Desire*, but it had
been published independently in 1947 by Losada in Buenos Aires. Of
its title Cernuda says in "History of a Book": "The conclusion of the
war reached me in Cambridge, and the title, *Like Someone Waiting
for the Dawn,* alludes to those years, since at that time it seemed
possible only to wait, to wait for the end of that retrocession to a
primitive world of obscurity and terror" *(PL*, 204). Certainly hope and
death are elements of considerable importance in a large number of
the poems in this sequence. In the face of such terrifying evidences of
chaos as those just witnessed in the Spanish Civil War and those in
the midst of which much of the civilized world still floundered,
Cernuda's poetry in this period is a labor of retrieval. He is deter-
mined to ransom out of his own past, his present, and the nature of his
art, a system of values, ethical and aesthetic, from which he can
contemplate disaster with some hope.

Cernuda will now turn to an examination of his art with greater
insistence in the spirit of "The Nightingale on the Stone" rather than
that of "To a Dead Poet" or "To L. with a Few Violets"; for, although
he continues to see poetry debased and ignored by the *vulgus,* he
considers it a necessary, intensely personal undertaking, not because
the poet must be defined in terms of society around him, but because
he must define himself apart from society. His judgment of poetry is
then a much more basic one; it is a judgment that reaches to the
source of his very awareness of himself. Poetry is, for Cernuda, an
ultimately ethical endeavor, in the traditional sense in which ethics is

70

a part of metaphysics and not in the pragmatic understanding of the term. His values are transcendent, not derived from social learning in the world at large or in the child's environment. His poem "La familia" ("The Family") attests to this very idea. The absolutes of nature, like myths, are expressions of a higher necessary order. They are the memories left by ancient gods whose search and invocation are ethically motivated as Cernuda understood them to be for Hölderlin. Furthermore, the poetic task is compelling not only because it is an affirmation of the unity of the self, but also because it is born of that inner drive, the "daimon" breathing with the poet, undeniable and ever-present in its questioning anguish.

The present man is but a product of his past, a trite though inescapable fact which Cernuda chooses to note in the last lines of "History of a Book": " . . . it was said already many centuries ago by someone infinitely wise: 'character is destiny' "[1] (PL, 216). The evidence of this consideration deprives it neither of force nor of actuality for the poet; he will frequently investigate his personal history because it contains the sources of his decision for poetry and because language can renew the past, can fixate the fleeting images of memory. Few poets have been as aware as Cernuda of the consequent relationship between our memory of ourselves and our sense of selfhood, of the increasing threat that time poses to our very identity, not merely in our future death but in our forgetting. That is why oblivion itself must become for him a species of memory and must be integrated into the present, to expand the minute point in time that this present is: the more we salvage, the more we are.

The present—reality around us—must be restructured and made part of our expanding self. Such is the sense of Cernuda's intense application of desire upon the world, upon time, as it arises from the poems of *Like Someone Waiting for the Dawn.* His relationship with matter and idea around him is an erotic one; it oscillates with the inescapable rhythms of passion, but like the forms it traces, it rises anew always. Ultimately, the impulse acquires greater importance than its object. For the poet sees desire as the form of his spirit, and its creations are then mere copies of this form. In such light the consideration of surrounding reality becomes increasingly abstract. Death itself is accidental to the essence of love, whose fulfillment is possible only in the throes of cosmic union. As we have seen, this search for the unity of inner and outer realities has remained a central element in Cernuda's poetry since *First Poems.* In *Like Someone Waiting for the Dawn* it finds expression and partial existential

success with "Vereda del cuco" ("The Cuckoo's Path") at the end of
the collection and is adumbrated in "Jardín" ("Garden") and "Río
Vespertino" ("Vespertine River").

We enter then with this collection a period of more philosophical
poetry than we have seen heretofore. This does not mean, however, that we are plunged entirely into a disembodied realm of
ideas. Cernuda remains true to that early tenet of always retaining an
"asidero plástico" ("plastic hold"); essence, in any case, is always for
him discoverable in circumstance. In this chapter we examine first of
all the poems of *Like Someone Waiting for the Dawn* that relate to
poetry itself and generally to art; in our next section we shall
emphasize the conflict—constant in Cernuda as we know and present
also therefore in other works which we may stress differently—of
desire and time. We shall concern ourselves thereafter with the
poet's meditations upon death and conclude with those compositions
where he attempts to express his intimations of cosmic unity.

II *Poetry*

Let us return once more as we look at those poems of this collection
involving the poet and his craft to that almost inevitable point of
departure for any consideration of Cernuda's main themes, his
statements on that "other reality," the true form of this reality and the
one that poetry seeks. *Ocnos* opens with a reflection on poetry
centering on this revalued reality: "I glimpsed then the existence of a
different reality from that perceived daily, and obscurely I felt
already how it was not sufficient for that other reality to be different,
but that something winged and divine must accompany it and halo it
as the tremulous nimbus that surrounds a luminous point."[2] Cernuda
remembers this childhood impression as an anticipating intuition of
his later understanding of what poetry does to life, that is, to our
dealing with *this* reality: "Thus . . . already appeared the magical
power that consoles life."[3] The magic of the poem should reveal that
divine nimbus, redeem in us the grossness of our daily contact with
this side of matter. It is not surprising that the poet should have
quoted in "History of a Book" from Massignon's book on Al-Hallaj.
For the Moslem saint's interpretation of reality and of our relationship to it is Cernuda's, too. The French scholar characterizes Al-
Hallaj as "a man of desire, eager to taste what subsists of things that
pass."[4] For Al-Hallaj this involves "a moral introspection of one's
self."[5] His mystical theology intuits the divine power as "an . . .
activity radically different from the sensible traces . . . that it leaves

engraved in our memory."[6] Finally, Massignon states: "If he directs through effusions of love all his desires toward God, it is to attest that the divine spirit alone can 'realize' these desires."[7] If we substitute "poetry" for "mystical theology" and refrain from personalizing the divinity, Cernuda's poetic vision is parallel to Al-Hallaj's theological one, even to the idea of "moral introspection" which, as we saw, is central to it. The search for the agreement of his inner moral self and the "divine" harmony, its union in fact, underpins much of Cernuda's work; this possibility sustains his life, directs his "desire"; and this realization maintains the poet in a constant adversary's position with respect to social man.

"Aplauso humano" ("Human Applause") does not deal with poetry alone, but rather with it as one of two main aspects of the poet's "difference," and with his pride in this difference. That the poet considers his separation from the mainstream of society a matter both poetic and sexual is made plain from the very first stanza:

> Now all those gray creatures,
> Whose meager love thirst is nightly satisfied
> By the conjugal milk and water, upon hearing
>   your verses
> May mock you because of the truth they expose.

"The truth" in this context is an erotic and simultaneously poetic truth quite unlike that of the "gray creatures." It is both of a different order and of a different intensity, for this desire is, by implication, altogether more demanding than their "meager love thirst." The following stanza reverses the emphasis:

> How many fashionable pedants and journalists
>   for sale
> Will then consider themselves the perfect
>   flower of humanity
> Next to you, as will the coarse churl
> Rooting *ad nauseam* in the dross of desire.

Now the distance between the poet and the others is born of the latter's vulgarity, and it is also a consequence of their limited intellectual perception of true desire. The next two stanzas link the truth of poetry and the truth of love—also, of course, his homosexuality— as necessary expressions of the speaker's self-understanding, that is, as they are now defined in terms of his own being rather than in contrast

with that of others. After considering whether this truth may not have
been debased by the mere fact of expression, the poet concludes that
his course was as inevitable and essential to his life as his very breath
so that he feels: "And if you hear a gibe, sudden as a stone/Let your
pride decipher in it the bitter form of praise" (RD, 216–17).

It is well to keep this piece and particularly its final lines in mind
when examining "Góngora." For some of the modern poet's traits are
equally those of his predecessor, and the poem appears then clearly
not only as an admiring remembrance of Góngora the man and the
poet but also as a projection by Cernuda of his situation into that of the
great ancestor—Don Luis de Góngora y Argote, Andalusian and
poet. Other parallelisms strengthen this assumption, for instance,
the specific decision to set Góngora in his self-imposed exile—
although it consisted in a return to his home in Córdoba and his
merely leaving the court, the fact of exile remains—within the more
general view of poets as outcasts in society or its victims (Lorca and
Larra were earlier instances in The Clouds). Too, similarities of
expression link both poems as reflections on a comparable plight,
such as in "Góngora" the lines, " . . . still reach him/The others'
stones, sad splashes/Of that slipslop dear for the people/Who compose the community, and as public are arbiters of glory."

The poem develops in five movements expressing Góngora's
greatness in contrast to his past and present evaluations by the
"community." The initial stanza situates the poet—"The Andalusian
grown old who has much reason for his pride/The poet whose lucid
word is like a diamond"—at the limits of his endurance of (1)
pervading indifference: "Weary of exhausting his hopes at the court";
(2) poverty: "Weary of his noble poverty"; (3) humiliation: "Weary of
soliciting favors from magnates"; (4) the failure of his fortunes away
from home: "Weary of the years so long misspent/In pursuing
fortune far from level Córdoba and its lofty wall." Stanza two shows
his decision to return to Córdoba arising from abandoned hope, "Now
he restores his soul to solitude, relying upon no one," and resignation
to his lot, "Now he resigns himself to see life passing as an inconsis-
tent dream." After this relation of Góngora's circumstances mostly
from the standpoint of his social aspirations, his character and position as a man, the third stanza ponders the highest expression of his
greatness, that of his work. Góngora's strength was in his poetry, and
it elevates him above all other, ultimately petty, difficulties: "But in
poetry he always found not so much beauty but courage,/The
strength to live freer and more proud." Yet even through this he was

destined to suffer, for "It is finally decreed that Góngora never was a poet/That he loved the obscure, and only vanity dictated his verses." But this too redounds to his credit, for it raises him even higher above pedestrian evaluations past and present: ". . . thus may/The very descendants of those who insulted him/Bow to his name, give prizes to the scholar,/Successor to the worm, gnawing at his memory." Such opportunistic reverence for the poet's genius merely reflects once more the insufficiency of his eulogizers now, as it did that of his detractors then, and he remains out of reach: "And he secured his irreducible soul/As an untractable demon laughing in the blackness."

The litanylike tone[8] and cadence of the poem with its repeated phrases and frequent recourse to longer lines give the poem unusual lyrical strength and a sustained thrust of irony. The recurring "Weary of. . ." in the first stanza intensifies Góngora's long-lasting but finally intolerable disgust at the futility of his endeavors, while, by implication, surrounding pettiness appears equally odious. In the fifth stanza the irony reaches its peak and the repetitions also accumulate in a final crescendo that borders on sarcasm: "Let us thank God for the peace of Góngora defeated;/Let us thank God for the peace of Góngora exalted;/Let us thank God, who knew to return him (as he will us),/Annulled at last, finally tranquil, in the midst of his nothingness" (*RD*, 192–94).

The impulse to pursue the poetic task, thankless though it may seem at times, is as irresistible as the need for self-affirmation and can no more be negated than can life itself. In "Noche del hombre y su demonio" ("A Man's Night with his Demon"), Cernuda explores that need to speak when everything seems to prove speech fruitless, when the temptation to cease is greatest. The poem is a dialogue between "the man" and his "demon" on the relative values of life and poetry, the "demon" intimating that in his devotion to language, "the man" has let life pass him by. We note first of all, as did Silver,[9] although he did not pursue the point, that "the man" and not the poet converses with his devil. Cernuda has gone here to the very heart of his being where the poetic impulse is separable from the self, since he sees precisely his devil as the source of this impulse—"Who else but you set that madness in me?" Cernuda comments on this demonic power in "Words before a Reading": "Confused with the lyrical gift that dwelled in certain poets, it seems as if their physical strength could not resist it [the demonic power], and they see themselves dragged to destruction, to find at last, beyond death, an enigmatic freedom."[10] This fate, which he attributes to Hölderlin, is the same one con-

templated in this poem. To the demon's accusation of having devoted
too much of his being to "the word," the man replies:

> Today you chide me for my creed of words.
> Who but you set that madness in me?
> The bitter pleasure of turning action
> Into sound, replacing deed with word,
> Has been the constant struggle of my life.
> And my unheeded, or barely heeded
> Voice, shall sound even when I am dead,
> Alone, like the wind among the rushes.

Words allow actions to subsist when their speaker has died. They are
the poet's strength and hope. But even this the demon denies:

> No one heeds a voice, as well you know.
> Whoever listened to another's voice,
> When pure and alone? The glib buffoon
> And vapid hierophant see their lies greeted
> By crowds' acclaim. They live, they prosper;
> You languish alone. Who cares for tomorrow?
> When fate forgets them and remembers you
> As just a name, a sound, a breath of air.

And yet the demon owes his existence to the man's very anguish:
". . . and you would not exist/Were I another, perhaps happier
man." The poem ends on a mutual realization of interdependence
between man and demon, the latter concluding: ". . . stand up, look
about you/In hope, though you can expect nothing here." For
ultimately eventual recognition is not a sufficient reason for the poet's
work, as he admits: "My pretense was guileless and hurt no one/But
myself, although this I knew at times"; nor is it enough "[To assume]
for others the conscience/Made supine in them, and their remorse,/
[To accept] the sins which they reject." Beyond all this, poetry is
essential because through it the poet finds "It is better to live amid
anguish/Than to dwell in ignorance" (PC, 106–13).

Not merely is it through poetry that for Cernuda life becomes
justified; through it one also finds knowledge in the sense given by
the ancients to the Greek term "gnosis." Thus, poetry becomes a
communication from the elements, so that the poet is a receptacle of
such knowledge and must seek it within himself, within his poetic
impulse. Such are the connotations of "El arpa" ("The Harp"), an

affirmative consideration by Cernuda of his art that speaks of the work's existential significance. As Silver[11] has shown, the harp is here a metaphor for the poet, the "invisible bird" is his inspiration:

> Cage of an invisible bird
> Brother of the water and the air
> Whose voice is solicited
> By the soft deliberate hand.
> . . . .
> What fruits of paradise
> What heavenly cisterns
> Nurture your voice? Tell me, sing
> Bird of the harp, oh lyre.
>
> (*RD*, 203)

While the poet's inspiration—"bird," "lyre"—is presented as descending upon him from the spheres, his role is not merely receptive. The "bird" will sing only when a "soft, deliberate hand" solicits it; "deliberate" for restraint and control, "soft" for delicacy. The communications from "the water" and "the air" must be formed as water is to become a fountain of life, as air is to become life or song. Inspiration may be an external force, but it is only the force; it needs to be shaped. What is available through poetry is more an awareness, a receptivity, which, when informed with the body of knowledge and art of the poet, may produce heightened moments of "gnosis," such as that intimated in the following lines from "Mañanas de verano" ("Summer Mornings") in *Ocnos:* "It seemed as if his senses, and through them his body, were a tense and propitious instrument for the world to render its rarely perceived melody. But the child did not consider strange that precious gift of feeling in harmony with life and that life should brim over in him, transporting and transmuting him."[12]

III *Desire versus Time*

Such plenitude may be invoked, but only rarely is it achieved; time stands as ever in the way, making experience inescapably ephemeral. There remains, as we have seen, glimpsed and struggled for, the possibility of going beyond duration and the intuition of a latent reality, both being essential elements of the desired consonance. This preoccupation, constant in Cernuda's poetry, was dealt with in the last chapter. Our intent here is to emphasize the change of mood that

has taken place in *Like Someone Waiting for the Dawn,* wherein a
more confident tone prevails and eventual fulfillment is even thought
possible.

"Las ruinas" ("The Ruins"), second poem of the collection, is a
meditation on the paradox of man's mortality and his ability to create
lasting beauty. As Coleman has indicated,[13] there is a clear reminiscence in the poem's opening of Rodrigo Caro's "A las ruinas de
Itálica," but, whereas Caro's work remains within the limits of a
reflection of man's passing, Cernuda pursues his thought toward
affirming both the necessity and sufficiency of beauty to sustain man's
and particularly the poet's self-assertion. Here, as elsewhere, God is
denied any significance except as an invention of man to placate his
fear of the unknown.

The early stanzas of the poem situate the ruins alongside perennial
events of nature. The ruins, too, continue, an expression of man's
dreams and of his thirst for the eternal, resisting time, holding it
through their beauty: "The marble ruins/Are a beautiful, musical
edifice/Made whole by a dream." These thoughts are followed by a
contrast between the durable remains of man's ancient greatness and
his own total disappearance. To all his endeavors there remains a
monument:

> The stones that living feet trod
> Centuries ago, remain still motionless
> In their place, and the columns in the square
> That witnessed the politicians' struggles,
> And the altars where they sacrificed and hoped,
> And the walls that veiled the pleasures of
>   the flesh.

The ruins, an external concretization of time, are but the tangible
form of the enemy man bears within: "They in whose mind eternity is
conceived,/Have within them, like a fruit's pit, death." The ruins
have captured time, and as man's frail bodies dissolve around their
core of death so have they left them behind. The reflection now turns
to God as the source of death and time as well as that of man's notion of
the eternal and more specifically the poet's:

> Oh God. You who have made us to die,
> Why did you fill us with the thirst
> For eternity that creates the poet?
> Can you allow the sons of light to fall,

> Century after century, into the greedy shadow
> Like thistledown blown away on the wind?

The last three lines of this stanza clearly set this putative deity's power in doubt, since, as opposed to the remaining constructions of man— "That titanic aqueduct's dry broken arches/Stride across the untilled valley"—he lets his own creatures disappear, frail "thistledown." The next stanza draws the inevitable conclusion: "But you do not exist. You are only the name/Man gives to his fear and impotence." Even though the beauty he creates may not last forever in its concreteness, the poet's vision of its eternal qualities is a sufficient bulwark against death. The poet has learned in his meditation that ephemeral beauty is beauty still, and more worthy of his desire than "Deaf, eternal gods." "Such is man" in strophe three referred to the ruins that remained as the sum of man's existence, monuments to his death. "Such is man" in the penultimate strophe refers to his awareness of the importance of life, the need to create and to enjoy beauty, because it passes as we do but continues to be more essential than the gods. The poem ends in a mood of calm acceptance as the poet surrenders to the propitiousness of the hour and of the setting: ". . . I now lie back/To gaze in peace at the landscape and the ruins" (*PC*, 88–93).

The powers of desire over our past are limited, however, in that there is bound to remain an unresolvable, undeniable core of experience which may be liable to reinterpretation, but not of total regeneration. We are thrown into the world of flux and subjected to it irrevocably, as are all things when they pass from the potential to the actual. The more individualized objects, beings, and events are, the more they are vulnerable to time. Potentiality is therefore preferable to actuality as youth is to maturity. Such is the assertion of "Juventud" ("Youth"):

> Rather than the spoken word,
> The silence that cradles it.
> Not passion—the dream
> Wherein it is latent.

> (*PC*, 94–95)

Here we approach such total solipsism that the poetic impulse seems endangered. But this potential lies within desire in the form of poetic imagination—in a sense reminiscent of Coleridge—and in the struggle

between containment and expression, desire, to exist, must choose
the latter. Yet is must choose such expression as will come closest
to its very essence which partakes of the eternal harmony, the love
that lasts. It needs but the barest of elements; thus "Ofrenda"
("Oblation") concludes:

> Such poverty is pleasing to heaven:
> Leave to the gods in oblation,
> As the living seed that is sown,
> The nakedness of your desire.
>
> (RD, 190)

The world of imagination and dream may remain, of course, untouched by time, more compelling for the poet. As we indicated,
greater differentiation implies a greater subjection to time so that in
fact there is a loss of absolute value. In "El brezal" ("The Heath") from
Ocnos we read: "Time, though it gave color, took away enchantment,
and much time had already passed, as you confronted your own
intimate reality with the other. So many things was the heath able to
say to you then, and now that you had it there, it was inexpressive and
mute."[14] The personal world of the poet is most completely lived in
imagination. In childhood, also, desire is closest to its pure constitu-
tive elements. Undoubtedly, that Edenic season exerts considerable
attraction for Cernuda throughout his life, as Silver has shown in his
excellent study. Yet childhood is not always remembered in a nimbus
of innocence or felicity. Already then the poet felt marked by his
difference, unable to belong to the very circle of his kin. There is no
real bitterness in Cernuda's apparent indictment of his family in "The
Family," merely sadness, for the parents could not have known how
unlike their wishes was their son, inured from birth to all traditional
injunctions, how their measured affection was to seem parsimonious
or even irrelevant.

The poem is a second-person address by the poet to himself, urging
the recall of those bygone days. This second-person technique is not
infrequent in Cernuda, as seen in *Like Someone Waiting for the
Dawn,* and there are two instances of it in *The Clouds:* "Evening in
the Cathedral" and "Alegría de la soledad" ("Happiness of Solitude").
Alexander Coleman[15] includes this type of dialogue among the many
aspects of Cernuda's projected voice, his "dramatic" poetry, while for
José Olivio Jiménez, it allows the poet to sing "from the deepest dregs
of his solitude."[16] The use of the "tú" form (literally, "thou," rendered

"you") implies, of course, that some discoveries are being made with regard to this projected "persona"; as Coleman says, it and the other "voices" of Cernuda's poetry evidence an increasing didacticism. There are other consequences that one may draw from the use of "tú": this teaching situation is aimed at the self, it is as if one part of Cernuda were lending the ability to speak to another, mute part of himself.[17]

This work is then best read as a species of interrogation, and indeed it opens with a question: "Do you remember, remember still that scene/Where you sat patiently day after day/In your childhood, remote now like a dream at dawn?" The repetition of "remember," meant to awaken the memory of that somewhat recalcitrant "you," underlines the difficulty of the recall. This initial question is wholly concerned with the effort to penetrate that monotonous—"day after day"—vivid, and yet unreal past—"Like a dream at dawn." The stage in which the remembrance will be played back is now set:

> The heavy silence, the drawn curtains,
> The circle of light around the dining table,
> As solemn as an altar, where there sat
> That family conclave, praised by so many before,
> Although you, less tenderhearted, have not yet done so.

An impression of oppressive ceremony arises from this description—"heavy silence," "drawn curtains," "solemn as an altar," and "family conclave"; the last line returns to the unwillingness to remember which must now be overcome. "Less tenderhearted" sets the speaker apart not only within the family circle, but apart also from those others who "praised" such scenes. It also prepares us for the cold backward glance by referring to the former refusal to celebrate. The scene chosen to illustrate the past is the family dinner, accustomed epitome of homely accord and warmth. It is a cold ritual: "Fragile and unyielding, like glass, /Which anyone can break, but none can bend." The comparison to the mass, to another ritual supper, underlying this family scene, infers in the context of Cernuda's work the same repetition of gestures that have lost their meaning, the same invocation of a unity and love that does not exist because its original intent has been forgotten or has drowned under the weight of solemn tradition. Things are done and responsibilities carried out with meaningless punctiliousness, a defense against the void. The child resists because his instinct for the broad generosity of true love and the vigor to see clearly can submit to no empty obligations:

But there was something else, huddled
Inside you, like a beast in its dark lair,
Which they did not give you, and this is what you are:
Strength of my solitude, I shall live in you,
Finding your truth through your mistakes,
Just as water springs and runs free,
Untrammeled by the need to turn machines,
Unchanging down to the sea, which is its destiny.
That love of theirs held you fast,
Like a garment made for someone else,
And that generosity, which sought
To buy your consent to anything
That did not accord with your nature.
You learnt then to hate that love which does not know
How to burn unknown without reward.

Together with this realization of his past strength, there arises
greater indulgence toward the family's shortcomings. In answer to
the empty rite at the dinner table, the speaker concludes with his own
prayer, born of an understanding he now extends to those who lacked
it then:

... may the gates of hell
Not prevail over you nor the products of your flesh,
Silent father, who never came to know your son,
Sad mother, who never understood him.

May those distant shades be not disturbed
In the uttermost limbo of the void
By their memory of you, like a pang of remorse.
May this ghostly gathering that invokes them,
Offering your blood like a libation
To make the departed visible for a moment,
Bring peace and pardon to you and to them.

(PC, 96–101)

The poem has been an iteration of those long-forgotten suppers, the
celebration of one mass whose significance has not been lost, where
the sacrificed son offers himself to redeem those who bore him and
bring them to life once more. From a delving into this cold and
adamant past, the poet returns with that clearer understanding which
demands the offer of himself as an atonement for the sins of others.

In *Like Someone Waiting for the Dawn* desire acquires its full
significance as both the origin of the poet's anguish in the face of flux

and the impulse to overcome it; it is the source of poetry. The son in "The Family" rekindles for an instant the life of his kin through his poem by filling with his substance the emptiness behind their gestures, creating out of his all-embracing desire, out of the "difference" that their regimented loves ignored, the justification they had not found.

IV *Serenity Before Death*

In his essay on Jorge Manrique, Cernuda says: "Death is not something different from life, it is an integral part of it, whose very perfection is achieved in death, without which life would have no more sense than an idle play of lights and shadows."[18] This attitude toward his own extinction has now replaced the despairing confrontation therewith which sounded through *The Clouds* as a persistent knell. The increased objectivity of tone in the later collection affects also the poet's view of death and leads him to structure the poems where it plays a major role as speculations on its significance, rather than emotive reactions to it. There is a gain in intellectual acquaintance with death's complexion accompanied frequently by a marked simplicity of language and anticipating the spare vigor of *Living Without Being Alive* and *With Time Running Out*.

In "Elegía anticipada" ("Anticipated Elegy"), an approximation of love to death elicits serene resignation. As the evocation of a cemetery, the piece is in sharp contrast to earlier treatments of the same theme; where death stood alone, stark and unforgiving, it now beckons, should the body return to earth in that same place where it met with love: "That is why memory returns today / To that cemetery, to the sea, the rock / In the southern coast; man wants / To fall where love was his one day" (*RD*, 215–16). Because death joins love in an affirmation of the apex of life, its contemplation no longer brings despair: "Of the intention that many may put into his actions, by referring intentions and actions to death, is born his immortality. . . . This does not surmise a negation of life, to which would inevitably lead the exclusive Christian conception of our existence; it is merely its serene affirmation."[19] Thus in "Hacia la tierra" ("Toward the Earth"), as in "Anticipated Elegy," through the interchangeable characteristics discovered in love and death, the latter is elevated to a new plane, becoming desirable; it is an object of love or the finality where oblivion may turn to love once more:

> But the soul must return
> As a bird in autumn,
> And that past sorrow
> Visit, and that joy
> . . . .
> Tired of sad dreams
> And deliriums,
> To return to its own
> Ancient dwelling . . .
>
> (RD, 217–18)

More frequently, however, the anticipation of death retains all its painful connotations, albeit now somewhat less harsh. In "Otros tulipanes amarillos" ("Other Yellow Tulips"), a reflection on the fragile transitoriness of existence, death is merely oblivion:

> Our life seems to be here: with leaves
> Secure in their branch, until the cold is born;
> With flowers in its stem, until the wind grows;
> With light there in its sky, until clouds surge.
> Perhaps for a moment you believed yourself certain
> In the world of man, were it not
> For that other world of the shadows
> Consuming the body as a waning moon.
>
> (RD, 219–20)

Death appears here muted because it is not a cessation, but a transition. That is to say, death occurs because something begins to "grow" instead of life. In a striking correlative arrangement we have:

	(leaves	The cold is born)	
ending	(flowers	The wind grows)	beginning
	(light	clouds surge)	

From "leaves" to "light" there is an increase in the brightness that ends; from "is born" to "surge" there is an intensification in the action that begins. In the opposite direction "light," although brighter, is more ethereal than "leaves"; "clouds," although of greater mass, are less sharp than "cold." The final image of the stanza presents the approach of death likewise as the growth of other elements, in this case the "world of the shadows," that is, for Cernuda, oblivion. Thus is death changed from an ending to a beginning, from a decrease to an

increase and back again, transformed also into interplays of light and
shadow, form and indefiniteness, and so diluted that its impact
disappears, absorbed by the mobility of metaphors.

The narrative poem, "Quetzalcóatl" (the name of a Mexican deity),
allows Cernuda to examine the approach of death from a completely
objective point of view, in that he has chosen as speaker an old
soldier, a man of both a different age and a temperament generally
unlike his own. Although the piece seems not to involve the theme of
death to any particular extent, hidden as it is under the epic matter
that accounts for the body of the tale, the examination of that theme
reveals an infrastructure not otherwise readily perceivable. The title
itself refers not only to the story of the God-king whose prophetic
arrival was fulfilled by Cortés but also to its mythical significance as
plumed serpent. According to Erich Neumann: "Wherever the night
sea voyage in pursuit of the sun is undertaken, by the gods or the
human soul, it signifies the development toward the relative inde-
pendence of an ego endowed with such attributes as free will. This
tendency . . . achieves its highest form in the myth of Quetzalcóatl,
the Mexican hero figure. . . . In his dual nature, he combines the
western, deathly aspect and the eastern aspect of life: he is the
evening star and the morning star. As morning star, he is the positive
symbol of the ascending power belonging to the male-spiritual aspect
of heaven and the sun."[20] There are two visions that meet in the poem,
although they are presented from the sole point of view of the old
soldier. The first one is that of the Aztecs, who believed that Cortés
was the God-king, come from the east, the morning star, bringer of
life and new civilization. The other is that of the soldier's, who looked
upon the appearance of Montezuma—evening star—as a miracle and
on the Spaniards' victory also as a miracle. The poem unites both
aspects of Quetzalcóatl as life bringer and death dealer; but seen from
the threshold of death and in terms of blood and conquest, the
morning star, bringer of life, becomes in the poem a bringer of death.

This conjunction is intimated from the start as the soldier begins his
tale: "I was there, but do not ask me / Whence or how it came, know
only / That I was there too, the time of the miracle." He looks back on
that double prodigy, both the appearance and destruction of the king
Montezuma. Old world miracles are replaced by those of the new
world, old legends by new ones: ". . . as thirsty, sandy ground drinks
water, / Thus did my mind imbibe the legends / Of those who moved
to the Indies." A transfer of allegiance takes place as soon as the coast
of the ancient homeland begins to fade: ". . . I felt yielding the

invisible knot/That ties us to our land." Immediately as he lands on
the new continent, the speaker meets with the first embodiment of
the myth: "Treading new land, destiny led me plainly/By the hand to
the man intended/For the feat: that Cortés, demon or angel." Like
Quetzalcóatl, Cortés unites within him life and death; he is first
described in images of light, in terms of Quetzalcóatl's configuration
as a star: "Temper of diamond, which is congealed fire/That blinds
the sight of those who look upon it." Now there enters again the idea
of predestination, the planned convergence of events toward a fated
goal held by myth: "The city, contemplated from the mountain,/
Unveils the secret intention of its streets./Thought an aimless confu-
sion when stepping upon it;/Thus did time unveil those our years/
Preliminary, though they had seemed wasted." The final expedition
by sea is now undertaken, the one leading to the central encounter
and which, as Neumann indicates, is part of the myth of the hero king:
"And so came the moment when we went,/A handful of men, across
the sea." The tale of conquest previous to the meeting with the Aztec
king follows. The stanza preceding this moment presents death at its
most pervasive: "I assaulted bodies, tearing out their souls/Hardly
tired of life,/. . ./I cut the flower of destinies in bloom." Under the
onslaught of death, art itself gives way: "Was there ever some
Garcilaso sunk/To the bottom of death by my stone?/Neither is of
this world, the kingdom of the poet."

The appearance of that other aspect of the god contains a reference
to the plumed serpent and is likewise presented in terms of revelation
and light. This is the moment anticipated in the opening strophe:

> When of a morning, through the arches and doors
> That the conquered capital opened before us,
> Undulated as a serpent of bronze and diamond
> The procession with a litter carrying the Aztec king,
> The very veil of the last heavens seemed
> To tear, glory now was bared.
> Yes, I was there, and I saw it; envy me, you others.

Here is the miracle of the new king replacing the old one,
Quetzalcóatl replacing another god-king, Christ, and like him, sacrificed. The final irony is in the triumph of death: "Now friends and
enemies are dead/And the dust of both lies in peace." The civilization
that has been introduced is a dead one: "Nothing remains to be done
today; bound is the land,/Which the trafficker claims as his/Trading
with bodies and souls." The myth was replayed, and death ultimately

won as it always does: "Of the wind the god was born and he returned to the wind, / That made of me a feather in its wings. / Oh land of death, where is thy victory?"

There is, in fact, no real exchange of myths, for Quetzalcòatl is but another aspect of the perennial sacrificial hero king, of which Christ also was one. Cortés's fate also is finally the same as that of his victim, Montezuma. The narrator is himself near his end, but he sees it from the vantage point of past glory and accepts it with calm: "And in a corner in the sun of this ground, mine more / Than is that other one abroad in the old world, alone, poor / As I came, I await at last without fear or hurry" (*RD*, 208–12).

In this many-layered composition, Cernuda has investigated death's most terrible aspect, one to which even art appears vulnerable, but also its most fertile one, for art in fact has integrated and transcended it. The poem uses a relatively recent historical fact, presents it in the guise of legend and pursues it to its mythical origins. Cernuda reaches back to an old-world myth of sacrifice and revitalizes it by uniting it with its new-world counterpart. Death emerges the victor as darkness absorbs the light-bearing god. But the original darkness was in fact the source of this light and only takes back its own. The uroboric mother contains life and death, light and darkness. Cernuda's consideration of death becomes thereby a source of poetry, just as reality, that is temporality, is the source of desire.

V   *The Search for Unity*

Although the poet's desire is awakened by his own individual encounter with the world and would seem therefore to be born exclusively of himself, it is for him, as we have seen, the expression of a cosmic force. This is not to say that the poet acts merely as the instrument of a higher order of things, the voice of the gods, as it were, in the sense of Plato's *Ion*. For the specifically poetic manifestation of desire is his own, as is likewise his own the very realization of this relationship between his particular erotic consciousness and the universal love-harmony. The difficulty of attuning the parcel of love that he possesses with the vast body whence it originates is caused by the discord between his duration and that of the world around him. This is why poetry is an essential element in the search for such consonance. It is born of the same impulse, and within the limitations of art it creates lasting moments of harmony. It is also the only possible medium to convey the mystical experience, although it must often be content merely to intimate it.

As we indicated earlier,[21] the experience of transcendent tranquillity may be either partial or total. It is partial when certain specific circumstances, essential to its occurrence, are felt to be by their very nature limiting and temporary, so that the event itself is but an adumbration of the greater concordance. The early walled garden of *First Poems* provided such a setting, and we find a similar experience described in the "Garden" of the present collection:

> From a corner seated,
> Look at the light, the grass,
> The trunks, the mossy
> Stone that measures time
>
> At the sun in the arbor
> And the waterlilies, flakes
> Of sleep on the motionless
> Water of the fountain.
>
> Up high the translucent
> Web of leaves,
> The sky with its pale
> Blue, the white clouds.
>
> A blackbird sweetly
> Sings, as the very voice
> Of the garden speaking to you.
> In the quiet hour
>
> Look well with your eyes,
> As if you caressed
> Everything. You owe gratitude
> For such pure peacefulness,
>
> Free of joy and sorrow,
> In the light, because soon,
> As you from here, it leaves.
> Afar you listen
>
> To the illusory step
> Of time, moving
> Toward the winter. Then
> Your thought and this
>
> Garden you thus contemplate

Transfixed by light
Will lie with long
Sleep, mute, somber.

(*RD*, 194–95)

Once more we note the "you" form of address, which suggests from the beginning a somewhat didactic intent in the poem: the speaker enjoins himself to do certain things in order that some knowledge be gained—as can be seen in stanza one. The principal act is one of contemplation; a quiet look from a sedentary position, in a "corner," so that all is visible without the need of any disturbing movement. The objects of examination are given in a gradation from circumambient "light" to the central solidity of "the mossy stone." This stone itself is a correlative of the whole poem, a softened hardness whose purpose—a further level of centrality, as it were—is to measure time. At the heart is unyielding time. The second stanza indicates that the stone is in fact in the center of the garden, itself a living, soft environment marking time, containing death at its core. Already this cyclical death is anticipated in "flakes of dream" with its suggestion of the winter's flakes of snow. The immobility is here suspended duration on the verge of movement. After this look level with the ground, the gaze moves upward in stanza three. There are no sharp contours or colors; this is an autumn sky. "The white clouds" against the sky are like the "waterlilies" on the motionless pond: both pass. The immobility of the water has transferred itself upward; the whole is in suspended animation. The fourth strophe introduces life at the middle level. The appearance of the blackbird begins the very gradual transition to the speaker himself, next to appear. This bird has a special significance for Cernuda. He dedicates to it one entire prose poem in *Ocnos*, where we read: "From the air it brings to earth some divine seed."[22] In "The Consonance", the last piece of *Ocnos*, he says "The bat and the blackbird can contend in turn for dominion over your spirit; at times northerly. . . ; others southerly, merry sunny. . . ."[23] In this stanza the blackbird too is a reminder of temporality at the center, however, and the total harmony is finally impeded.

Although the first line of stanza five reiterates the advice of the poem's opening, to look, it begins the moment of interpretation. The importance of the senses is amplified; one must look with one's eyes, not merely in imagination; one must accumulate these perceptions, in anticipation of their later disappearance. The gift of the garden to

the observer ("the very voice . . . to you") is now returned to it ("as if
. . . gratitude"). As the scenery is interiorized, the tempo of its
changing is increased to that of the observer's duration in stanza six.
Likewise, the flow of the poem has accelerated. The first and second
stanzas were linked syntactically as if following the movement of the
speaker's gaze and suggesting the initial, almost heedless absorption
of the scenery. But calm asserts itself quickly and two full stops curb
the opening rush at the end of strophes two and three. With the
appearance of greater movement and the anticipation of the speaker's
role, stanza four is also linked with five; and from now on they all glide
into one another until the end. The syntactical bonds between
strophes five and six, and six and seven, are the strongest in the
poem, a verb and its object, an adjective and its noun. Temporality
in all its mobile decay penetrates stanza seven. The steps of time,
though illusory, prove stronger than the real presence of the garden,
carrying all with them to the end, forward into the future (stanza
seven). Man is pierced through with time as the garden itself is
"Transfixed by light." Man and garden have become one, both
bearing within the "mossy stone that measures time." Light will
become darkness, communication will end, all will be "mute,
somber." The separation at the opening of the poem between the
garden and the observer has dissolved. But the merging takes place as
a realization of mutual temporality, the speaker bearing with him
toward the "long sleep" the quietude of the scenery. It is a merging
penetrated by time. The speaker is within the garden as the garden
comes to be within himself, and both are contained by time.

The serenity achieved in "Vespertine River" is fuller, though also
ephemeral. It is reached through the poet's own willed abstraction
from the course of events through invoking his role as their judge and
interpreter. Exceptionally in Cernuda, for a work of this length—
ninety-four lines—the poem does not fall into a stanzaic pattern; it
flows in an unbroken monologue, an image of the flow of the river and
of the history it traces. As it opens, the poet walks to the banks of the
river:

> Leaving behind the cloister, wherein sound
> Echoes of new and latent voices
> By the old mill path
> The river is reached, . . .
> . . . .
> All is abstracted in a pause
> Of silence and quietude. Only a blackbird

> Makes the evening shiver with song.
> Its destiny is purer than that of the man
> Who sings for man. . . ."

We meet immediately with three types of singers: those in the cloister away from the stream of life; the blackbird favored by the poet, as we have seen, and here envied by him; and the poet himself. At this point the voices in the cloister and the bird's song enjoy a fate superior to that of the poet—he is *away* from the cloister *beneath* the bird—for his duty is to be the "signifying voice of the flock" and therefore he remains caught in the river of time. The poem will reflect his gradual ascent to the level of the other two voices until he replaces them and gains temporarily the freedom and solace that is theirs.

The poet sees first his task as a burden: "Condemning the poet and his task/Of seeing dispersed being in unity." But in consideration of this task, inevitably he begins to separate himself from "the others" for he has remained true to the role that he must play while they have betrayed theirs: "The profound meaning of work/Remains disregarded by the others." Yet he still feels that some recognition should be given to the poet. Soon, however, he sees that too great an attachment to this world is time misspent: "Existence does not matter, nor the time/Given to justify it, thus one dies/Not of a present but a future death." All values have been distorted; the poet reaches here his bleakest moment: " . . . wherever the eyes look/Only memory of death do they find."[24] Hope rises anew, and one must deny the demands of a sterile though evident earth and place one's faith in the unseen:

> . . . The earth demands
> Too much, and the air is generous.
> . . . .
> Faith, against all reason, is a blind thing
> A shadow quieting thought.
> If the voice of the poet be not heard
> Is it not a better fate for the poet?

The poet has raised himself above the turbulence of history and present decline, finding peace in this indefinite moment of dusk:

> Man learns language from man,
> But he learns silence only in God.

> In the vespertine peace, humbler
> Than animal jubilation in the morning,
> What was renounced is now possessed,
> When the light finally laid down its sword
> In that time without time, consummating
> The identity of day and night.
> The ghostly wind among the elms
> Moves the leaves gone and those to come.
> The blackbird is asleep. The stars
> Do not yet descend to the water.

(RD, 225–28)

The poem's end answers its beginning, all other voices are quiet except the poet's in an interval of pure present.

The tacit eloquence of water, now a quiet pool, prompts also the introspection of "Vereda del cuco" ("The Cuckoo's Path"). In his own reflection, the poet remembers, he first glimpsed the form of a greater all-encompassing love. The poem uses again self-address as a maieutic technique to recover the past or rather to integrate past and present selves. We can therefore expect some gain in knowledge or understanding to have taken place at the conclusion of the poem. In this sense, we may discover a basic organizing principle in the reasoning that transforms the situation of the beginning into that of the end. The poem opens with the idea of search and discovery:

> How often have you gone in another time
> This fountain's way,
> Seeking along the dark path
> Where the water surges,
> To remain immobile at its margin,
> Watching with mute amazement
> How there, amid the depths
> With similar though remote gesture
> Appeared another semblance
> Of inevitable enchantment,
> Propitious and adverse,
> And you contemplated it,
> As he who contemplates
> Destiny unfolding
> Upon the sand in mutable signs.

The present remembrance, as that original search "[on] the dark path," is to come face to face with that image. Its past contemplation, as if it were destiny, is paralleled by the present memory of that contemplation, inferring endless self-reflections wherein lies that destiny. This multiplicity of mirror images is of course continued in the very *dédoublement* represented by the "you" voice. At that time there was only the appearance of another, reflected in the pool, both similar and remote because his significance was as yet unfathomed. But while the surface meaning of the strophe offers us merely this duality of the self, the implied meaning already suggests a potential multiplicity: we have the present consideration of a past self observing its own image, pondering its destiny, that is to say, its future image, and so on.

If our reading is correct, the actual surface duality should have achieved its hidden, potential multiplicity at the end of the poem. The last strophe reads: "Although your day has passed/It is you, and those gone,/Who seek through these new eyes/In the face of the fountain/The deep reality/Intimate and enduring." In effect, the youth and his image are now "you, and those gone." The initial tentative self-love has grown and propagated endlessly while turning into certainty; the quest has found its object, and early indecisive desire has become a powerful affirmative love. At the same time, what began as the physical evidence of an image—"there surged another appearance"—has achieved the intellectual certainty of the *real*—"the deep reality." The beginning of this last stanza refers to the speaker's past, relative to his present: "Although your day has passed/It is you and those gone,/Who seek. . . ." What the poem has done is to spend that past, to relive it as the new truth was being discovered. The speaker's entire life is summarized by those walks to the pond, source of desire and of its realization.

The initial four stanzas, which concern the first stage of love, when still regarded in its physical aspect, begin with the *action* of going to the site: (1) "How many times you have gone . . ."; (2) "An atavistic desiring attracted you/Here . . ./. . ./And indecisive your pace stopped"; (3) ". . . the man whom you already were/Went to the spring"; (4) "How many times did you step/On this dark path." Consequent with this pattern, the imagery in the four strophes is generally physical—with slightly metaphysical suggestions in the last lines, a point we shall return to below. Thus the first stanza makes a general statement about the frequency of the event, the walk to the pond. The second recalls the original occurrence in adolescence. In the third stanza it is the man's turn to go. The fourth stanza, as the one concluding this first part of the poem, is an echo of the opening one and evokes all those past journeys.

The next stage of love's progress, the mystical stage (examined below), has been prepared carefully in that each stanza progresses from the physical act of approaching the actual source to a more intellectual consideration of the source's significance. The indefinite reminiscence of the first stanza becomes at its end a musing on destiny. Similarly, the conclusions of stanzas two and three speculate, respectively, on the contradictions of desire and on the prison of desire. Stanza four ends with an intuition of the nature of love: "For love is eternal, and not what is loved."

The transformation of love into mystical communion is achieved in the second part of the poem in four stanzas where the imagery is less concrete. Their design, however, is parallel to that of the preceding group of strophes. The fifth one—corresponding to the first— through general approximations of the essence of love reaches the apex of mystical transport in language reminiscent of that of St. John of the Cross. The sixth strophe returns to more individual references, although of an abstract nature, and sees the body and its personal desire in the context of a greater whole; the seventh views other young bodies as replicas of the speaker's own past self, their passion a twin of his own. The last stanza, in an echo of the fourth *and* of the first, situates the journey to the fountain in the context of life's search for ultimate satisfaction, endlessly begun. All stanzas have remained analogous in structure, as we see, for instance, in the fifth which we quote at length since it sings the instant of mystical joy:

> For it to be lost,
> For it to be won
> By its passion, a risk
> Where he risks more who loves more,
> Love is the source of all;
> There is jubilation in light because that
>   fountain shines,
> The wheat spike contains god because that
>   fountain flows,
> Words are a pure voice because that fountain sounds,
> And death is its covetable bed.
> Ecstatic on its margin,
> Oh divine torment
> Oh divine delight,
> You drank from your thirst and the fountain at once,
> Your thirst and the water tasting of eternity.

> (*RD*, 229–32)

The passion, risk, and love of the beginning become the taste of eternity.

Each stanza has moved within its own realm of imagery from containment to extension. The entire poem develops from a remembrance of past concrete events to a metaphysical deliberation on their significance. The initial fact of narcissistic self-discovery and desire becomes the discovery and desire by the speaker of others, and the discovery and desire by the many of the many; the self multiplies endlessly. In addition, the concrete fact of physical attraction, of passion circumscribed, surpasses its limits and is transformed first into the delight of mystical union and then into the intellectual awareness of its compelling nature.

The meditation points to the possibility of transcendence for the poet and traces back to its origin the rise of his desire; youthful narcissism is but the seed. Self-love grows, multiplies itself, overcomes time and space when it gains this knowledge.[25] In this poem, one of Cernuda's greatest, a temporary solution is offered to the main problems faced in *Like Someone Waiting for the Dawn:* they are the same as always—desire, time, and death. Nor is their solution new. The quasi-mystical awareness was conceived before and actively sought. But so complete an integration of past efforts to this end had not yet been reached. Death itself is now bathed in the aura that emanates from such desire and *is* desirable when it is a road to unity. The solution is ephemeral in that this state of communion is experienced but rarely; the poet's daily existence and daily passion, the material of his work, while retaining an echo of the cosmic order, are imperfect means of reaching it.

CHAPTER 5

Living Without Being Alive: *The Weight of Years Past*

I *Introduction*

THIS collection of poems was begun by Cernuda in Cambridge (during 1944–1945), continued in London, where the poet settled in 1945 to teach at the Spanish Institute, and completed at Mount Holyoke College in the United States in 1949. In "History of a Book" Cernuda situates at this point in his reminiscence some of his most important commentaries—previously quoted in part—on the direction toward ever greater simplicity that his verse was taking. He signals his continued search for straightforward expression aiming "to employ, within my intention and purpose, that is to say, with fitness and precision, terms of daily usage: the spoken language and colloquial tone towards which I believe I have always tended" (*PL*, 205). He also underlines here his search for a muted rhythm: "If there is music in verse, my preference has always been oriented toward the 'quiet music' in it" (*PL*, 205).

The very title of this book of poems stresses the disjunction within the poet's condition. At this moment of incipient middle age, Cernuda feels the weight of his past clearly impeding his view of future days and becomes intent on reorganizing it poetically. He will turn a searching gaze toward his former self. But his questions will merely make more evident, more inescapable, what was already intuited: time, while offering the illusion of a constant flow, is in fact as discontinuous as the contingent reality wherein it seems most clearly manifest.

Consistent with this investigation of the years behind him, Cernuda will frequently[1] choose the *autodiálogo* (a dialogue with the self) or "you" address whose importance we noted in *Like Someone*

Waiting for the Dawn. Such interrogations should lead to a greater understanding of the past or of the present and the future in terms of this past, always with the aim of achieving a more complete definition of the poet's entire being. Also, time, his constant antagonist, will gain even greater importance. It hides the true complexion of the past and erodes the borders of the present. It affects, as always, the poet's capacity to love and hides from him the sought-for unity. In this chapter we shall examine the poems of *Vivir sin estar viviendo (Living Without Being Alive)* from three principal viewpoints, all related to the temporal experience: time and love, time and the self, and man and nature as discrepant temporal cycles.

II   *Time and Love*

As we have seen, love for Cernuda is a transcendent as much as a physical need. Already in his earlier work it almost invariably burst through incidental circumscriptions to acquire a clear metaphysical import. At this point in his career, the significance of erotic sentiment is for the poet almost wholly spiritual. To recapitulate, it is now possible to say that love uncovers the true reality of the universe, because it shows the unity that underlies apparent dispersion; the poet sees in its force the great creative impulse at the origin of things, physically *and* poetically.

Through his love meditations in this collection of poems, Cernuda undertakes a labor of discovery. The effort of remembrance, for him basically an effort of self-definition as we suggested in our last chapter, will focus on moments of love or on the memory of its occurrence because they are moments of deepest intensity. They are those instants of greatest self-realization and consequently, those also of greatest realization for him of reality because highlighted by desire. In like manner, as the identity of the universe is visible in the love-harmony that moves it, so is the identity of the self through time perceivable, established through the reliving of past erotic moments and through their reintegration. The quartet that opens *Living Without Being Alive* is an examination of love in precisely such a temporal context; the counterpoint between love's origin in time and its nature as the echo of a supratemporal reality is underlined by each one of the "Poemas para una sombra" ("Poems for a Shadow"). They follow the four principal moments of erotic realization: birth-spring; maturity-fall; waning-winter; and apparent death in the final poem "El fuego" ("The Fire"), which obviates the yearly cycle.

"La ventana" ("The Window") presents the reawakening of love as
a penetration of light into the mind of the lover. This illumination
redefines reality and time, returning to them an essence lost during
the loveless interval. Love begins by fanning the interior flame,
thence to project itself upon the lover's surroundings, revealing to
him their true nature:

> Remember the window
> Above the nocturnal,
> Almost monastic garden; that dark human sound
> Of the leaves, when time,
> Full of the beloved presence and figure,
> An immobile wing above eternity,
> Already turns your life
> Into the cordial center of the world,
> Oblivious to yourself
> Alienated among things.
>
> All splendor, a spring mystery,
> The sky glows
> As water cooling in the night air;
> And contemplating it, you feel
> Sorrow in abandoning this window,
> To cede so much life to sleep,
> The body anticipating
> The definitive repose
> When through love your spirit ransoms
> The deep reality.

The first stanza invites a merging of past and present—"Remember,"
"Already turns"—as well as an initial thrust toward the unity that the
loved one creates among things—"that dark human sound of
leaves"—and the consequent surpassing of time. The introspection
begun at the window expands first, and then through the intercession
of the loved one's presence, plunges to the heart of the lover, now the
core of the world. Individual qualities, specific objects, become
manifestations of the external thrust of love. The second stanza
follows a similar development, but begins now at an already exalted
circle of reality, the simile "sky = water" intimating the total union
that is being effected through light—"splendor," "glows". The position already gained the "cordial center of the world" allows now for a
vision of "The deep reality." Stanza three reveals the newly found
vigor of the soul in love, a vigor which stanza four recognizes as born

of submission to the light in the eyes of the beloved. The fifth stanza contains the central thought of the composition in its six final lines:

> It is the gaze which creates,
> Through love, the world,
> And love which perceives,
> Within dark man, the divine being,
> Creature of light, alive then
> In the eyes that see and understand.

The crucial importance given to the eyes, to light, throughout the poem reaches its first peak here where the gaze creates the world. In stanza seven, the love born in that gaze has become "A fixed star illuminating time" and extends its empire from the world of matter to the world of time.[2] At the end of the poem, the dawn and the light in the eyes of the beloved are one; both illuminate the world:

> While you contemplate, now at dawn
> The pure and deep blue of those eyes
> So that always night
> May be illumined with your love.
>
> (RD, 235–37)

Love recaptured in the spring is as light renewing the soul. The concluding image makes of love's birth the birth of the day, of love's light the light of creation out of darkness.

The second poem of the quartet, "El amigo" ("The Friend"), considers the powers of love when its object is no longer pursued. Its beginning ponders the effect of the lover's absence in terms reminiscent of the preceding text: "But he is not here, nor the light, nor the leaves." It is now autumn; the unity of things achieved before seems lost; nature is mute and blind at midday: "Now noon, with its sky/Approaching, veiled/The river of blind waters." The lover will find no answer in the outside world, but within himself the presence of the beloved has grown with remembrance; both are truly one: "Do not seek him outside. He can no longer/Be distinct from you, nor can you/Be distinct from him: you go united" (*RD*, 237–38).

In Poem III, "La escarcha" ("The Frost"), Cernuda's meditation follows a pattern similar to that of the previous two poems, a pattern which we recognize almost invariably in his reflexive verse: from the apparent concreteness of reality, he moves to a realm of abstractions where qualities are no longer physical but moral and relationships no

longer spatial but intellectual. The transition "exterior—interior" is
in this case rather quick. After a rapid glance at the frost on the trees,
the mind veers immediately toward subjective evaluations:

> Look at the trees, as in summer,
> By frost budded
> With leaves once more, frozen leaves,
> Spectre of those gone. Thus to the mind
> Does that image of love, friendly before
> Now return a stranger.

The thematic continuity linking these poems into a unit as love
meditations finds its correlative in the recurring imagery of trees and
leaves with which the entire sequence was begun, appearing early in
each piece. In this as in the previous composition, the negative
connotations of the opening statements, the strong reminder of the
beloved's absence found in the setting from which the reflection takes
its departure, are destined to disappear as the poem proceeds inward
where love remains alive. In this sense the "you" address again plays
its heuristic role: the poet-as-speaker guides that more impulsive part
of himself away from the evidence of the senses to that of love's inner
light. The glowing center, however, proves more difficult to reach
every time. The struggle between heat and cold, light and darkness,
is not resolved here until the penultimate strophe. From the depths
within, the true direction is predicted away from the superficial
layers of the self that have remained vulnerable to appearances where
the voice may still be heard: "Against time, in time/Thus the mad
presage: 'Wait, wait' " (*RD*, 238–40).

The intense radiance of reborn love has become so integral a part of
the lover that it participates also in his ever-renewed fountain of
desire. This transformation announces the final one in "El fuego"
("The Fire"), the fourth composition. Using an elm as the image of his
love, the poet equates the fire it gives when turned into firewood with
the flame of desire that remains in the ultimate transubstantiation of
Eros; essential things always return though in different form:[3]

> Whatever destiny steals
> Is later recovered in strange form;
> To win, to lose, are senseless names:
> Look how your love, your tree,
> Are crowned with the flame of another impulse.

> (*RD*, 240–41)

"Four Poems for a Shadow" is a unitary composition in four parts whose central metaphorical developments are moments along the same axis. While this axis is temporal, it leads to an overcoming of time in the same manner that the imagery of ephemeral leaves becomes symbolic of the durability of love. The evolution of the leaf symbolism and that of the temporal connotations are both in their turn the supports, as it were, of a metaphorical sequence centered on the relationship between love and light as follows: (1) "The Window," spring—leaves in vigor, night illuminated by love: love=light; (2) "The Friend," autumn—leaves disappeared, light is fainter—loved one is "specter": love=sight: (3) "The Frost," winter—simulacrum of leaves by frost, light becomes a shadow: love=haze; (4) "The Fire," rebirth in fire—tree cut down—no possibility of leaves: light=fire, love=fire. Thus an echo of the first poem vibrates in the last with a return to the predominance of light; love is engendered in another avatar, now part of the poet's myth: ". . . the myth of your still incomplete existing" ("The Fire"; *RD*, 241).

The apparently final incarnation of love as mystical flame in life is in fact but a transitional phase in its transformations and anticipates the tension of desire toward an ultimate satisfaction beyond death that "El éxtasis" ("The Ecstasy") seeks to affirm. The title is referred by Cernuda himself[4] to Donne's "The Extasie" and indicates the kinship between both compositions; this kinship lies in the intimate relationship that each poem establishes between the mystical and the physical qualities of love as aspects of the same cosmic force. For Cernuda, however, the ecstasy is sought through union with that forgotten aspect of himself found in each love: "Unknown and known, with the charm/Of a rose that is itself and the memory of another rose." All the beloved resemble one another as they resemble also the lover. The surrender to love is likewise a merging with those aspects of oneself that have been forgotten and make for a discontinuous identity. Love is then both a subjection of the self and a means of recovering it in its wholeness. That is why many of the poems that seem to involve a delving into the past to seek the younger self could also be examined as variations on the theme of love. Now, however, our emphasis will lie mainly on the transformations of the poetic persona through time.

III   *Time and the Self*

As if his self had been dispersed through time, Cernuda searches his past for elements of his identity that would attenuate his feeling of incompletion, the formlessness that life seems to impose upon him. But his earlier self frequently proves either beyond reach or unrecognizable. The present remains unfulfilled, imprisoned in its separation. And yet from an impulse not unlike that which allows a glimpse of cosmic unity, though more limited in scope, there arises the possibility of joining the *personal* past and present toward a future that is hopeful because it is unknown or perhaps less painful.

The wrenching sensation of divorcement with which the poet lives arises not so much from the loss of substance of the past, a fact whose unavoidable evidence could be lived with, but from the intense desire driving him still to its recapture. We encounter here another aspect of the gap between reality and desire, and that reality already impenetrable then is all the more so now because chained in time to its past. The present self finds its identity undermined by this distance and this shield. In "El intruso" ("The Intruder") the poet's personality appears to break into fragments when faced with the disjointedness of time. Although still performing its quasi-didactic function, the second-person address in this poem increases further the dislocation of the ego; since the lesson that the speaker wants to teach to his projected persona involves inner discontinuity, the learning procedure itself becomes part of the knowledge gained. In the first three stanzas the discordant experience is defined as a lack of harmony between actual being and expected realizations: the life now lived seems a borrowed one, as if time had made some mistake. The center is pursued in passing external things and the confidence of youth, still awaited, is denied by the figure of the present self: "But your face, reflected / By some distorting mirror, old, / Sullen, far removed, breaks in / As an alien presence." The mirror image is as if multiplied by the adjectives that describe it and the distance between the two selves increases. The disconnection is complete in the last stanza:

> In order to reach the one who is not you,
> The one you are not guides you,
> While friend is stranger,
> And the rose is the thorn.

(PC, 115)

From questioning the authenticity of life, of circumstance, of interaction between the self and the world, the poem has uncovered the void at the heart of being. This doubting of intrinsic selfhood reverberates through the final metaphor to endanger also the web of the real: passing beauty becomes lasting pain.

The same effort to establish contact with youth dominates "La sombra" ("The Shadow"), although the questing glance begins nearer the poet's erotic core. The assimilation of the effort to recapture youth to the love experience stems from their similar significance in rising above time-laden reality: "On awakening from a dream, you seek / Your youth, as if it were the body / Of the comrade asleep / Next to you which you do not find at dawn." The dream or sleep from which one awakens into the world was that supratemporal plane of the erotic and of the penetration into the past: both suppose the possession of another body, that of the friend and that of youth, here one and the same. The absence of that body, the lost relatedness with past aspirations, relegates the self to the limitations of a present whose foundations shift to reveal emptiness again. They negate the possibility of completion at the most elementary level, the wholeness of being. This void is the more unrelenting when all awareness even of past illusions disappears and is merely "A vague malaise, an ignorance / Quieting the past, leaving indifferent / The other whom you are, without pain, without relief" (*RD*, 261–62). The youth, at first that other desired self, has plunged the present one also into alienness.

On other occasions the poet does not forget that " . . . on his youthfulness fed / That sharp pain . . ." ("The Shadow") and tries to reject the often unavailable and, when reached, often disappointing past. Still this rejection, opted for in the last resort, is tinged with regret. In "El prisionero" ("The Prisoner") one set of chains seems to have been exchanged for another; while the limitations of the past have given way to freedom, this freedom is ultimately cold isolation:

> But you won liberty
> With no one, and it seems to you
> A desolate victory,
> A figure of death.

> (*RD*, 244–45)

The decision to delve clear-eyed into the past which many of the poems of *Living Without Being Alive* exhibit, together with the growing use of objectification—dialogues with himself—and of dramatizations, reflects in Cernuda not only the pressing need to come to terms with hitherto unexplored aspects of his personality, but also the resolve to accept his entire condition. He looked upon the last half of his stay in England as a watershed period marking the second part of his journey toward death. At the same time, and in particular during the final years, he lived with the hope of complete change that his departure for the United States promised. In this time of transition an accommodation with the past had to be attained. It is just this kind of undeluded summing up that the doubly objective "Un contemporáneo" ("A Contemporary") offers. In this poem Cernuda uses the fiction of a relentless "contemporary" speaking of an acquaintance whose lot is unmistakeably the poet's. The tone is conversational, matter-of-fact, and the story is recounted with both indifference and dislike. But the reader soon wants to penetrate beyond this surface, and refuses to accept uncritically the given facts whose calculated colorlessness cannot prevent a hidden depth. The speaker's limitations become evident as he pontificates on literary matters, offering appreciations that run counter to experience:

> . . . Is it possible, then,
> For a future poet to live unknown?
> We know that a poet is something different.
> The spark that burns within him quickly catches
> Those who cross his path in life,
> . . . .
> Was there perhaps excess in the oblivion
> He lived through day after day? . . .
> . . . in death we take with us what we took
> From life or what it gave us: oblivion
> Here and oblivion there; it's all the same.

(PC, 116–23)

The last lines are a near admission of defeat. Negative evaluations of earlier days have created a void beneath the poet's present that seems at times, as in "A Contemporary," to deprive it of substance or at least to question its commitment. In such reduced circumstances, desire comes to be replaced by hope and produces a paradoxical return of expectations which had seemed to belong exclusively to youth, so that the willed casting off of the past allows for one of its strongest qualities to reemerge. "Otros aires" ("Other Airs") hopefully calls for a surrender to the potential of the future. The yearning for days to come attains unexpected vibrancy, if at first veiled under the cloak of idle musing: "What will those trees be like?" The poet links his renewal to that of the trees in winter's end, finding in them a correspondence to his inner world: " . . . and amid those trunks / You find your faithful world. . . ." Nature awakens to receive him and offer him renewal:

> A promise, do you hear?
> Is perhaps ringing with the nascent leaves,
> Its existence, like yours,
> In music hidden and revealed.

(RD, 262)

"Viendo volver" ("Seeing Return") is a most intense poem on the task of recapturing the past and in some ways resolves the problem. The poet begins with an unspoken premise that might be—were it possible: "You would go, and you would see/Everything the same, everything changed,/As you yourself are/The same and another. Is not a river/Each instant/Itself and different?" The old Heraclitean simile is formulated by Cernuda in its true sense and not in the one that we have come to accept and which we owe to Plato. The latter emphasizes the idea of change—" . . . you cannot go into the same river twice."[5] Heraclitus's text reads, however: "Upon those who step into the same rivers flow other and yet other waters."[6] Here the element stressed is the *identity* of the rivers. The rest of Cernuda's poem pursues the thought of sameness through transformation, defining the enduring of identity as that of desire through sight: "For looking is merely/The form in which persists/Past desire."[7]

Under the revealing gaze the self endures, though in separate, uncommunicating moments:

> You would see him, dreaming
> The future, without present,
> Awaiting the friend
> When the friend is himself and in himself
>   awaits him.

The present then was wasted in expectation; the present now turned to the past in remembrance undoes its own future:

> On seeing him, you would like
> To leave, alien then,
> With nothing to tell him,
> Thinking that life
> Was a delicate joke
> And that today the youth must ignore it.

(RD, 273–74)

The singularity sought in the past has remained only in the form of change, but it was necessary to lose in order to gain an understanding of the loss. That is why communication would remain impossible. The hopes of the past continue unanswered by a present whose essence is change; in like manner the past leaves unfulfilled the desire of the present, for that past must needs be different.

In his backward glance, Cernuda has tried to substitute memories for desire and found them wanting. When the poet accepts the irreconcilable discrepancy between the past and the present as an aspect of the perennial gap separating reality and desire, he also accepts the compartmental character of his "history." With this realization, his recollection becomes more objective. In "El retraído" ("The Introvert") memories are aesthetic toys, unreservedly available for poetic use in moments of meditation. Here too, as in the previous composition, desire is at the center of remembrance: "Turned toward yourself you pursue/The loving ramble/Of that which was as it should have been" (*RD*, 242–48).

IV *Time and Man, Time and Nature*

We know that intimacy is seldom absent from Cernuda's poetry, especially in those works that concern themselves with duration. Still, there are degrees of centrality allowed the poetic persona; whereas the poems examined so far in this chapter installed personal experience at the heart of their development, there remain a group of compositions where temporality is objectified and considered in terms of man in general or as displayed in nature. Two poems, "El árbol" ("The Tree") and "El nombre" ("The Name"), occupy a transitional space between man and nature. The tree in the poem bearing that title and spring, or April, in "The Name" become mediating ideas which allow the poet's reflection to focus on a singled-out youth in the first case and on the shaping process of the poem—therefore on the poet—in the second.

In "The Tree" there remains a demarcation between the natural object and man though the object stays as an available point of conjunction or as intercessor to a higher, perfect realm. It is there as a reminder, particularly to that youth who can feel its inner power. In this sense, the idea of mediation is pursued at two levels: the tree is intermediary to the intuitive youth, and he in his turn is intermediary to other men, those not possessed of his gift of sensitivity. The step that would make of this youth specifically a poet or *the* poet is possible but not necessary. Furthermore, a distance remains between the youth and the tree in that he too, with age, loses some of the capacity to "see" while the tree is unchanged.

As is customary in Cernuda's meditative compositions, the opening objective description contains within it the principal components of the speculation to follow:

> Next to the water stands, as a legend
> In its walled and silent garden,
> The handsome twice centenary tree,
> Its powerful extended branches,
> Compass of so much grass, interlacing leaves,
> Canopy wherein subsists an Edenic shadow.[8]

At first glance the tree seems characterized in straightforward terms: it is old—"as a legend," "twice centenary"; it is secluded—"walled," "silent"; it is beautiful, powerful, and vast. The last line, however, introduces with "Edenic shadow" a connotation giving another resonance to these qualities: the description is now charged with echoes of Genesis. The "legend" recalls that of the trees of life and knowledge. The situation of the sycamore "next to the waters" is not merely objective description; the spatial detail acquires defining force and makes of the tree of life the ancestor to this one which grows near life-giving water. The "walled garden" and the plane tree's age are the present, limited conditions of that previous occasion: immortality in Eden. They also imply the ideas of sanctuary and veneration. The tree's extension is a concretization of its age and power, while the intricacy of "interlacing leaves" maintains an air of mystery. All these connotations lead to the more directly mythical statement of the stanza's last line.

The next stanza pursues the determination of the poem's premises while beginning their development with regard particularly to space. A contrast is suggested between this northern plane tree and its southern "brother" under which ". . . it is pleasant/To let time die, divinely useless." There the tree's relationship is to a contemplative type of man, whose remembrance of Eden and the tree of life consists in "[letting] time die." As in the opening stanza the concepts of space and time are presented conjointly. In the next strophe the tree's renewal in spring is announced by a tentative burgeoning of flowers at its feet; its rebirth crowns that of nature. Youths arrive next, coming to the water in their own resurgence. Nature's participation in this life is seen as a tension of desire: "Trembling, so many light bodies, stays the water;/Vibrating, so many resonant voices, stays the air."

The next five strophes of the poem are devoted to man and in particular to that rare being who may, on occasion, feel within the tree "The sap's secret urgency, rising/As if it were the beating of his own destiny." As the tree stands, a living reminder of possible timelessness to this youth, so does he stand a mediator to other men by his intuition of the living myth of their own unmeasured, forgotten potential. This potential, though generally ignored, is closest to fulfillment while young. The growth of ignorance in man is traced in strophes six and seven; it is concurrent with the waning of their youth and with their enslavement to social custom, the trappings of temporality. But early enthusiasm and insight also fade somewhat in that rare individual who felt them strongest. Strophes eight and nine show him growing old, less responsive, a stranger to his younger being, his earlier quality reduced to the clear-eyed realization that from his spirit ". . . the fervor fled, changed to disgust, / As a displaced bird in the nest made by another." The tenth and final stanza returns to the tree's presence:

> While, in its garden, the handsome tree exists
> Free from the mortal error that engenders time,
> And if light escapes its summit in the evening,
> When shadows slowly overcome that air,
> It seems sad only to him who sadly sees it:
> Being of a perfect world where man is alien.
>
> (RD, 242–44)

These lines close the development initiated in the poem's opening: previously seen "as in its *walled* garden . . ." the tree actually ". . . exists/*Free* of the mortal error that engenders time." It now appears fully in contrast with the confined humans who contemplate it. The youth who felt his destiny linked in its plenitude to that of the tree is left with only the awareness of his loss, but his meditation may reawaken in us the memory of a perfect state to which the tree attests.

In "El nombre" ("The Name") temporary respite is achieved from the sensation of life passing through a delicate, unifying equilibrium between man and his surroundings. As usual, the event takes place in a natural environment. The speaker exhorts himself to become receptive to the quiet beauty of spring among the trees; as a "second-person" composition, it contains some didactic elements, although the lesson is to filter through the senses via aesthetic intuition rather than the intellect.

The poem opens with the entrance into an almost sacred zone, propitious for contemplation. The approach should be restrained:

> Let your step reach quietly
> Upon the earth where
> Shines with a red shadow
> That beech, and neighboring it
> With its shadow of gold
> That chestnut tree, to the touch
> Of the same light. . . .

The double meaning in Spanish of *tierra* as "earth" and "ground" expands the context of the first two lines. The walker's steps may be said to "reach" the "earth" as if it were a new arrival because the earth is now new in spring. Still, he is apart as yet from all around him, and other constituents of the scene also stand out individually; even the light—almost invariably an expression of harmony in Cernuda—acquires different qualities as it is absorbed by either the beech or the chestnut tree. The intruder is himself merely addressed in terms of his steps. The poem will now proceed to gather this dispersion until it can be contained within the spectator's mind and within one unspoken word—"April."

The first stage of unification is undertaken through time references. Personal time is abstracted from general duration: ". . . Pass/This hour with yourself/Alone, as if it were/A last hour/A first one. . . ." There has been a gain in the existential coherence of the onlooker; as meditation follows sight, his entire being is involved rather than a disembodied step. Corresponding to this attempt at cohesion, the outside world's time, hinted at previously as shadings of light, acquires its unitary compass: ". . . turns the afternoon/Of unutterable peace/And unutterable loveliness." The repetition of "unutterable" achieves, paradoxically through a word asserting the defeat of language, language's beginning containment.

The next stage develops the idea of appropriateness in nature: "The world is with its sky." Through its falling blossoms the apple tree reaches out to merge with space. The extension of grass elicits thoughts of lovemaking and the air breathed in brings delight. The man is brought to the first, physical state of conjunction: "Even the man/Yourself, quiet,/Seems, among the others,/One more tree. . . ." We enter now the moment of spiritual communion, born of that all important sense, sight: "Gather your soul and look;/Few look at the world." In a simile introducing once more the idea of desire, nature returns the loving gaze: "Reality by no one/Seen, patient awaits,/As a young being,/A mirror in eyes/Enamored. . . ." The last two elements that remained apart have merged in this instant:

> . . . all
> Human gesture turns
> Idle, and only a name
> Thought, but not uttered
> (April, April), perfectly
> Contains it and gives it
> Sole and sufficient form.
>
> (RD, 245–46)

The moment stands precarious on the edge of dissolution. It grows from unperformed action—"all . . . idle"—to unspoken word "Name . . . not uttered." Tacitly, language has abstracted man from time and joined him to nature in its youth, creating a new, combined totality. This unifying expansion belongs not to the real but to the re-creating power of words whose simplicity in this poem underlines even more clearly their effect.

V   Man's History

A comparable effort to allow language its power over temporality is recognizable in "Otras ruinas" ("Other Ruins"), a poem which may also serve as introduction to those in this collection that examine the intermittences of history and man's attempts to resolve them. With respect to Cernuda's own poetic journey, the piece highlights the creative continuity of his inspiration by recalling another poem with parallel title and subject; the poet throws a bridge across time in poetry and creates for the later work an ancestor whose echoes reverberate through the years. In this instance such continuity contrasts with the tone and content of both poems. "The Ruins" from the previous collection (see above pages 78–79) was a reflection on the power of beauty to resist time. "Other Ruins" castigates man's drive toward self-destruction exemplified in the massive sordidness that remains, after war, of his sterile edifices. As we return to the earlier poem, our reading has been tainted by that of the later one, and it is the past civilization's disappearance, rather than its remains, that strikes us now. For Cernuda, the more recent work situates the former in a long tradition of similar desolation that starts with the Bible: "The tower which they built with machines, /Through the agency of machines knows its ruins." The tower in question looks back to Babel and the fall of the first mythical civilization of city builders. The sole continuity is that established by human discourse, and it emphasizes destruction in the histories it produces.

In this composition Cernuda attributes man's suicidal bent to the exigencies of social organization, his incapacity to live alone—we remember that the first murderer was Cain, who tilled the soil and whose progeny were builders of cities; that his victim, Abel, was the shepherd, traditionally the self-sufficient, solitary man. The ruins are viewed in the light of the function which the original buildings performed. The inner incoherence which social custom hid as a thin veneer shows through in the ruins of man's most concrete creations: ". . . flight of stairs that leads to nothingness/Wherein its dwellers burst with stupefied gesture, /A game of hazard, without coherence of destiny." The city's destruction is but the latest instance of that lasting curse man brought upon himself when he forgot how to live alone; and he forgot his gods, also, for only in solitude does one meet with the divine: "For whomsoever knows how to live alone no longer, henceforth must he die alone. /The god's last gift to man is ruin" (*RD*, 249–51).

Because of the inability to rise above his earthbound, time-bound condition, ordinary man will misapprehend the past as he does his own present. In "Las edades" ("The Ages") this limitation works both ways: when a civilization perishes, its gods fall and become subject to temporality and decay because they are the creation of man and need him to remain in their heaven. Forgotten, they are:

> Tragically foreign, unfastened
> From their eternity among the stars
> Free from time, thus they appear today
> In Museums . . .

Such interdependency of man and his gods is not a new thought in Cernuda; it was central for instance in "Undertow in Sansueña." It reaches its clearest expression in this poem: "A people exists through its intuition of the divine."

The gods themselves attain their immortality because they are born of man's desire; man in his turn may also overcome his mortal condition by his commerce with the gods he has created. "The Ages" shows the results of the rupture of this bond in the condition of such gods, now corruptible as man:

> The carious rock, the corroded marble,
> Is decomposition of the god, certain
> To consummate itself beneath the air, as is
> Beneath the earth that of man.

But our admiration of their form without essence deprives them of the oblivion that is now their due. Unwilling to invest them with belief, men gaze at their beautiful decay: "And hostile as strangers they offend their agony / With an incredulous admiration" (RD, 259–60). As we know, Cernuda believes it is given to the poet, on occasion, to surpass the temporal and to see reflections of that other reality. Unfortunately, such moments of exaltation, infrequent though they are, by intimating that unity of being otherwise dispersed in isolated parcels of his past, render his more habitual residence in the limited present an imprisonment. His efforts to achieve consonance, however, are not in the nature of an escape from his usual condition; rather they represent attempts to organize it and control it, to find in it a form making it congruent *here* with those aspects of the world that respond to the perennial elements of reality, with reality's own shape. It is through the real and with its help that Cernuda seeks the higher harmony.

For Cernuda to structure reality means to elevate it from the formless to the formed and to save it from change, that is, from time. Poetry can do this. Power, political power in particular, has forever been exerted also to the same end. Unlikely as it may seem, it is possible for both activities to coincide in this purpose. Plato used both his literary and philosophical genius to erect a social structure immune to change, since for him change was necessarily decay. In "Silla del rey" ("Seat of the King") the poet explores the conscience of an absolute monarch who feels it within his grasp to arrest change—as well as decay, which also exemplifies a divergence from his norms—and deny time its outward expression.

Contemplating the building of the Escorial, Philip II reflects on the monastery's significance for him and for Spain. It is an edifice commemorating the changelessness in social and religious order inflicted upon a nation of extremes in character and dominions, whose newly won unity it symbolizes as a merging of opposites:

> In act and in idea already life adjusts itself
> To my catholic canon, through fields,
> Through cities, through seas passable
> To dark, discovered lands beyond,
> And man is free in me, as I am serf in him.

The true achievement of the king is not merely external unity but the inner harmony imposed upon his subjects, free to obey; he has shaped the eternal to his concept of form:

> My work is not without, but within,
> In the soul; and the soul, in the hazards
> Of good and evil, is equal to itself:
> It is neither born, nor dies. And this that I build
> Is not stone, but soul, the inextinguishable fire.

Philip II has created the concrete equivalent of that identity of opposites which according to Heraclitus underpins the world. By extinguishing change—"Mutation is my disquiet"—he maintains forever this harmony as its summit, solidifying duration in the image of the palace: "And the future shall be, immobile, the past:/Image of those walls in the water" (*RD*, 264–67).

The Escorial is the summation of a people's meeting with its god as are the statues of "The Ages." Such unity in faith provides a temporal stasis not unlike that achieved by the poet when he attains the elusive existential plenitude. The nation's past is finally seen organized toward this instant of fulfillment and becomes reincarnated in it. Contrary to the monarch's wishes, however, the instant will pass, as the waters will stir and undo the image they reflect. Later centuries isolated the moment in its apex of splendor and folly and showed no harmony containing these extremes. What remains of that thirst for immobility Cernuda states in the last lines of "Ser de Sansueña" ("To Be from Sansueña") referring to Spain and those forgers of passing glory:

> They lived death, yes, but with monstrous
> Glory. Today we die life
> In an alien corner. And meanwhile

The worms, from her and her irreparable ruin,
Grow, prosper.

To live to see this
To live to be this.

(RD, 263–64)

For the poet, ultimately, the past is not regained and should not be. As we saw in the earlier portion of this chapter, even as "pastness" it is useless. In this collection of poems, where the fullness of age induces Cernuda to look back and redefine his identity through former acts, the backward glance become poetry is exorcised. It is in the present that, as in "The Name," the tension of desire must be resolved.

CHAPTER 6

With Time Running Out: *Coming Home*

I *Introduction*

*C*ON *las horas contadas (With Time Running Out),* the penultimate work incorporated in *Reality and Desire,* was written in
the period from 1950 to 1956. It was begun at Mount Holyoke College
and completed in Mexico. There are two principal sections to this
sequence; the first consists of a series of poems on topics previously
dealt with by the poet and ranges from meditations on historical
events—For example, "Aguila y Rosa" ("Eagle and Rose") again on
Philip II—to evaluations of his own personal and poetic history.
These latter poems are imbued with the sense of pressing time
implied by the title of the book and which will continue into the next
and last collection. The second group of compositions, "Poemas para
un cuerpo" ("Poems for a Body"), are love poems, the crowning
moment of Cernuda's arduous quest for erotic fulfillment. They
represent the poet's "arrival home" in both the physical and spiritual
sense, first from the purely amorous standpoint, since these two
components of the love experience are inseparable in Cernuda and
second, from the more prosaic point of view of the recovery of a
homeland, the closest yet to his native Andalucía, in Mexico.

Cernuda's own commentary on *With Time Running Out,* after
stressing the idea of urgency that he wanted to capture in this title
regarding his concerns with time in general, as well as his love
experience, moves on to some more technical statements on form
which are of particular interest: "Most of the compositions that the
collection incorporates were less extensive than those of previous
collections and among its verses appeared assonant rhyme, indicating
on the one hand the search, perhaps not always conscious, of how to

LUIS CERNUDA

concentrate the theme, rather than to explore its ramifications and on the other, the tendency to song. Neither thing was always the result of a voluntary decision; rather often they originated from a subconscious impulse" (PL, 214).

The United States seems to have left little imprint on this group of Cernuda's poems. His residence here was anticipated as a liberation in one or two compositions from *Living Without Being Alive*—"Other Airs", for example—but after visits to Mexico it is to this country that his mind turns as to another, truer home. From his memories of the stay at Mount Holyoke stand out two main points: one is a student's heartfelt suggestion that he not remain; the other, his discovery of pre-Socratic philosophy through the reading of Diels' *Fragmente der Vorsokratiker* and Burnet's *Early Greek Philosophy*. It was inevitable that a nature so sensitive to the environment as Cernuda's should find the northern climate of Massachusetts unbearable after the sun of Mexico at the end of almost twenty years of exile.

The theme of exile and its end makes itself felt in the very first poem of *With Time Running Out*, "Eagle and Rose," belonging to the trilogy on Philip II. Set in the monarch's youth, it recalls his arrival in England and short-lived marriage to Mary Tudor and his return, alone, to Spain. Central to the composition is the idea of infertility; the first line announces the expectations that promoted the alliance: "What the great-grandfather sowed, the father wants to reap"; these expectations were to remain unrealized as Mary is left alone in England. The opposition, fruitfulness-sterility, is set as light against shadow: " . . . But her life has known, / If not the flower, its shadow." Thus Philip (the Eagle[1] = light) arrives on the island with the summer, and his sojourn there will be short as this English season is for a Spaniard. The Rose (Mary) although ultimately sterile will have enjoyed the light of the sun and known its shadow, their dead child. Philip's departure is not exclusively linked to the marriage's failure, but also to his realization that "Tasks and affections are not ours / If we find them in a land that is not ours" (RD, 281–84). Such was to be the poet's condition until his departure from the Anglo-Saxon world and his settling in Mexico, the sufficient and final "homecoming."

Two poems in particular signal in this collection the importance of this homecoming in terms of the climate and the contour of Mexico, so similar for Cernuda to his beloved Andalucía. In "El viajero" ("The Traveler") there is first wonder in the experience of another climate:

"It's you who's breathing/This warm night air/Among the evergreen leaves." This forgotten mildness amid new, lasting greenery imposes itself with greater evidence than the traveler's own self-awareness of which he must remind himself. The intuition of belonging will grow slowly; initial surprise will soon become recognition while the body's sense of fitness with the surroundings prefigures the merging of previously sundered inner realities:

> At last your dream coincides
> With your truth, try to forget
> This truth's fragile, even
> More fragile than that dream.
>
> (*PC*, 139)

In "País" ("Country") the principal components of existence for the poet are recalled from the standpoint of their "country" of origin. Through the idea of displacement, the outline of a spiritual mother-land is traced in which physical realities contribute their adequacy to the spirit:

> Your eyes are from where
> Snow has not stained
> Light and among the palm trees
> The air
> Is invisibly clear.

Light and the eyes are mentioned first because they are for Cernuda necessary conduits of the soul. The second term in the delineation is desire in its elemental, physical manifestation, uniting: "Animality with the secret/Grace/Of glance and smile." These elements, when properly attuned, constitute an existence from whose margin may be perceived: "Eternity in time" (*RD*, 295).

The acute importance for the poet of ambiance and landscape achieves here one of its clearest expositions and renders fully the necessity of his departure for Mexico. The finally encountered congruence of spirit and environment is an aspect of the ever sought reciprocity between reality and desire, and announces the more encompassing fulfillment of love to be expressed in "Poems for a Body." But as if in preparation for this event, under the pall of pressing time, Cernuda continues to take stock of his condition as a man and as a poet.

II A Chosen Path: The Man

Of "Nocturno yanqui" ("Yankee Nocturne"),[2] one of the major poems in "With Time Running Out," J. Olivio Jiménez says: "The harsh history of his ethical projections (the incorruptible sense of dignity, the anxious search for his truth, or for truth, loyalty to his own destiny) is here told with virile soberness without personal profuseness, with an expressive concentration that avoids the slightest shadow of languor or dejection."[3] The search for the elusive image of himself in the past, already qualified in several poems of *Living Without Being Alive,* has given way to an objective realization that such a meeting could not be, that the poet's present self is also his past self and contains it, that the choices were his and he made them. The poem's rhythm, recalling that of Manrique's *Coplas,* introduces the depth of cultural reminiscence and his own creative past by evoking other works where similar links were elicited. (We saw another instance of this effect with "Other Ruins" in our last chapter.) In accord with the objectivity of Cernuda's self-analysis, as well as with his goal of clarity, the language is bare, the tone plain and untrammeled.

The development in Cernuda's meditative works from material to abstract evidence follows from his evaluation of reality according to a different plane of being; but whereas in many cases this plane of being was of a vaster, different order, it is found now within the poet as a simple and direct apprehension of continuity. The restrictive view-point adopted here adds the element of irony to that of self-examination which generally flows from the use of the second-person form of address also chosen for this meditation.

The poem begins with a detached consideration of the surround-ings; but the objectivity is only apparent, for each stanza transforms its central impression into nascent thought. Thus the first one:

> The lamp-light and drawn curtain
> Shut out the darkened town.
> Dream now,
> If you can, if you are content
> With dreams, when you lack
> Realities.

After the rapid strokes circumscribing the space wherein the poem's action—strictly mental—is to take place, the gaze turns within immediately. The opening two lines describe both an illumination and a veiling that may be taken as objective correlatives of the work's central discovery, in that the final awareness is a self-appraisal involving the acceptance of a loss. At the same time, the double movement of the gaze without-within, concrete-mental, parallels that of the whole poem and is repeated by each stanza with slight transformations, to provide another instance, even at this superficial level, of the great structural cohesiveness so frequent in Cernuda. The retraction of the gaze toward the inner world is markedly ironical, as will be the gradual plumbing toward the center pursued by the poem to the end. Considering that Cernuda's activity to this time has consisted precisely of a turning toward the self and that the poem considers now the sense of this activity, the undertone of irony is doubly suggestive as an evaluation of his life's work in purely existential terms. It is a measure of the objectivity he has attained that he can integrate such an evaluation, accept it as a fact and continue nonetheless.

The poet is led to consider aspects of time in two main steps: (1) objective time—watch, seasons, time spent in reading; already with the thought of books enters that of memory and the new understanding of once-read texts; (2) personal duration—(a) as the filling of the present; a first blush of realization at the core appears now: "Life is lived in time. / Your eternity is now"; (b) as the painful memory of the past. Time is then examined in terms of the necessity which absorbed most of it: teaching. The significance of such work is quickly dismissed: "No one can teach what matters, / A man has to learn that / On his own."

The final stanzas proceed to values more central to the poet. His search for love appears an affirmation of the self, the crucible of his integrity, demanding special inner strength also because Cernuda's was a homosexual passion, socially stigmatized. This awareness allows him to say: "And you found who you were." The truth of the self, through the pursuit of personal values, is the truth of the present containing all before it:

> You are now what your life was;
> You are not one without the other,
> You know that.
> And you must carry on then,
> Still after the lost mirage,
> Until the day
> When the story comes to an end,
> For you at least.

And so you think
That you are back
Where you were at the start
Of your soliloquy: alone
With yourself.

Put out the light and go to bed.

(*PC*, 126–35)

All realities and attentions which had previously stood in the way of dispassionate appraisal have been dismissed; the poet finds himself with his own truth though it brings little comfort. The deliberately prosaic conclusion returns to the equally objective beginning in a slightly ironic underplaying of the meditation by "lamplight," incidental, so to speak, to daily waking and sleep. Perhaps now in bed, the dreaming, suggested in the first stanza and interrupted by the reflection, will in fact take place. It is paradoxically now when he is able to see his past with greater coolness, when he sees it more plainly, that the poet feels able to reacquire that capacity to look ahead which he thought belonged exclusively to his youth.

Previous backward glances sought a past that would respond to the ideals maturity heaped upon it. It proved inaccessible, and the failure of the search threatened both the present and the future. Now, as in "Lo mas frágil es lo que dura" ("It is Fragile Things that Last"), youth seems merely confident expectation: "When time would one day soon/In that future fulfill/Your every desire" (*PC*, 144–45). Youth's mark upon the present is "a smell of orange blossoms," an image of what it was, sensual anticipation at its most indistinct. The past's reduction in significance allows memory to approach its reality more closely.

At other times, as in "Otra fecha" ("Another Date"), the present, while it offers nothing certain, does not need to look back:

In your more than precarious today
You miss nothing former,
For what is gone is well gone,
As what is dead is well dead.
(*RD*, 301)

Rejecting years gone by as useless ballast does not, however, guarantee that those to come hold so great a promise. Yet, to meet squarely even the uncertainty of the time he feels "running out," he needs more than ever the inner conjunction toward which his meditations have tended in various ways and which he saw, for instance, in Gide, of whom he says: "His entire life coincided with him, / Every promise equal to every reality" ("In Memoriam, A. G."; *RD*, 292). As Gide did, Cernuda must find satisfaction with his chosen path as a man and also as a poet.

III A Chosen Path: The Poet

Cernuda feels at times that the dilemma of needing, as a poet, the recognition of society while also as a poet rejecting its values, will forever remain insurmountable. In his authenticity he disperses throughout his work essential aspects of himself and his vision which, he fears, will be either ignored or misunderstood, a thought that leads him in "Soledades" ("Solitudes"), for instance, to question the worth not only of his enterprise but of himself:

> Why do you leave your verses
> Little though they may be worth
> To people who are worth less?
>
> You yourself, who say it so,
> Are worth less than anyone,
> Since you did not learn to be silent.
>
>   (*RD*, 300)

That the acquisitiveness of the powerful should at times dictate the ultimate destiny of poetry elicits in the poet a reaction of unusual bitterness at this stage of his work and makes of "Limbo" the most somber of his compositions in *With Time Running Out*. At a social function the poet hears the offhand remark: ". . . 'They offered me / The first edition of an odd poet, / And I bought it.' " In the poem's setting this statement becomes a complete, though perhaps unintended disparagement of the poetic task. Here also, as in "Solitudes," the debasement of poetry reflects on the poet who was unable to take a stand against formal constraints in order to defend his art.

From the beginning of the poem, the truth of nature is itself veiled to the eyes. The winter square where stands the house in which the reception takes place "Seemed not reality, but a sad copy / Without reality . . . ," under the snow and the gray sky. The poet has a premonition of his fate: "Living here you would be / The ghost of yourself." Inside the house, darkness reigns, colors are tamed and hidden "In a Spanish tableau, in a French / canvas. . . ." The host sits next to his own portrait as if he felt that the reproduction increased his being. In the midst of this artificiality, mention is off-handedly made of the "odd poet" by one of the numerous madeup women or socially correct men. The statement itself reveals the value placed on the poetry to be minimal, emphasizing the commercial aspect of the transaction—"offered," "first edition," "I bought it"; the writer and his work are lost in the exchange. This is his final death, his work ". . . another vain object,/Another useless ornament." The strongest accusation falls on the visitor himself: "And you coward, mute/You took leave then as one who assents." The ambiance has transformed him also, turned another poet into a diminished replica of himself, manifesting thus the sharpest instance of its power. He feels violated beyond the grave: "Better destruction, fire" (*RD*, 297–98).

Cernuda holds no illusions as to the poet's destiny and that of his work in our world. We know this to have been a strong, early realization that continued throughout his writing. But two central considerations sustained him against all odds, both aspects of his ethical stance: first, poetry was for him a deep expression of the self that he could not and would not deny; second, he felt that it was not given him to deny poetry because it chose him, just as he chose it. Refusing its call would have been similar to willfully shutting his eyes, walking as a blind man while blessed with sight. The concept of the poet as the instrument of a higher will reappears with the same force as before—for example, "The Harp" (*RD*, 203)—in "Instrumento músico" ("Musical Instrument"):

> To awaken the word,
> The feather of which bird
> Grazed by which hand
> Is the one that wounds you?
>
> (*RD*, 288)

The vicissitudes of this combat with the demands of poetry are quickly retraced in "La poesía" ("Poetry"); quickly, because the battle was won from the earliest by the stronger force and the man only, not the poet, occasionally questioned the harsh submission. It was a short-lived questioning, as in her wisdom the mistress knew it would be: ". . . poor in everything without you,/To your voice calling, or its dream,/Alive in his servitude he answered 'Madam' " (*RD*, 298–99).

In the interesting poem "Retrato de poeta (Fray H. F. Paravicino, por el Greco)" ("Poet's Portrait [Fray H. F. Paravicino, by El Greco]"), [4] Cernuda joins to the condition of outcast that of the poet as instrument of a displaced language. In a now uncommon first-person reflection Cernuda addresses Paravicino as a brother poet and a brother in exile—as he had Góngora—the portrait of the Golden Age preacher finally becoming Cernuda's own. The poem opens with the similarities linking the two men, both being exiled for similar reasons: ". . . Who brought you/The madness of our people, which is our own,/As it did me? Or greed. . . ." Paravicino looks back "To that stopped time . . ." when language reached its height, when he employed it to inculcate the truths of the soul on his restive compatriots: "The very things that sustain your life,/Like that land, its oaks, its rocks,/Which there you look at calmly."

At this moment of the meditation the agreement between present and past poets ceases, for those things speak no more to the man of today: "I do not see them . . ./. . . In yesteryear's nests/There are no birds, my friend. . . ." The present poet's solitude is greater, since he has lost the ancient faith, even though the force of the language remains. The final stanza returns to common elements in their mutual exile and the implied accusation directed at the mother country; the poem concludes with two lines that join this general condition to that of the poet: "I? The gentle and animated instrument,/An echo here of our sadnesses" (RD, 288–91). Thus a poem that begins as a meditation on the portrait of Paravicino turns to thoughts by its writer on his own fate; while reaffirming the intent to pursue his devotion to the language, last, irreducible inheritance from Spain, Cernuda lays at his country's feet in a sad but mild indictment the responsibility for that plight.

Cernuda's evaluation of his work has not altered significantly in this sequence of poems. Poetry remains, with love, the most essential affirmation of his being; it generally sustains him in his bitterest moments and keeps alive his hopes. But we have seen it falter once or twice; certain situations, for instance, when the thought of speaking in a void imposed itself upon him, led him almost to the denial of poetry's ultimate value—for example, "Limbo" and "Solitudes." It is time for the other cordial component of his being, desire, to re-awaken. The resurgency of love is anticipated in "Pasatiempo" ("Pastime") as that event able to support him when the very memory of the homeland becomes faint, or when the fate of his writing seems endangered: "Your work, paid in secret/With coin on wind/By the

few." In these bleakest moments the hope of erotic completion
continues: "Hope that from some hazard/A young body may be/
Pretext in your existence" (RD, 296–97).

IV Love's Affirmation

In the poem "Después" ("Afterward") nature in spring portends a
general rebirth of desire, but as youth awakens to the fire of renewed
blood and the body prepares to surge again, the poet sees himself
excluded from the general metamorphosis: "But you, shadow without
body/. . ./Yet you, shadow without desire" (RD, 296–96). These two
lines (written in italic script) stand in contrast to the rest of the
composition, unassimilated elements in its forward movement. Soon,
however, circumstances were to prove the poet wrong and revivify,
in experience turned to poetry, the adamant core of desire remaining
within.

As Cernuda recalls in "History of a Book," the sequence of "Poems
for a Body" was occasioned by an actual encounter in Mexico during
his visit there in the summer of 1951. He was aware of the possible
ridicule to which his condition of *viejo enamorado* ("ageing lover"), as
he terms it himself, exposed him, but he also knew " . . . how there
are moments in life which demand from us the surrender to destiny,
total and without reservations, the jump into the void, trusting in the
impossible so as not to break our head. I believe that at no other time
was I, if not so much in love, so well in love, as may perhaps be
glimpsed in the verses . . . that gave expression to the said belated
experience" (PL, 211).

The sequence consists of sixteen poems describing various aspects
of Cernuda's experience of love. In spite of the earthliness which the
title would lead us to expect, they deal almost exclusively with the
inner lineaments of the poet's desire and range from an almost
Platonic communion of souls to the concept of the loved one as a
catalyst for the poet's erotic potential. The body is metaphor more
than physical presence. It becomes simply the "loved one" and
reaches its greatest actualization perhaps in the first poem entitled
"Salvador," (literally "Savior" as well) should we accept that such is,
in fact, the beloved's real name. Similarly, the most concrete assertion of the poet's own existence occurs when he discards his literary
persona to become "I, this Luis Cernuda" in Poem III. As we shall
see, in both instances, the "naming" arose from textural necessity.

It is significant that in this, one of the most poignant periods of

Cernuda's poetic career, he should have abandoned his "expository" style in favor of a shorter, more intense lyrical form with the reappearance of assonance (see the quotation of page 115). Of course, if we take the entire sequence of "Poems for a Body" as a meditation on love, its individual poems appear as specific moments of coalescence in need of no further development. The intellect plays a lesser part here, not in the sense that the artist's control over his material diminishes in any way, but rather in that discursive reasoning has disappeared. Absent likewise, except for two instances—Poems II and IV—is the self-address technique; this results in a natural way because the sundering within the poet's being has been largely resolved for the moment. The lover may find his existence reduced to the point of reification as is the case in the first lyric, "Salvador." Even so, there is no self-interrogation toward discovery; logic is now of little use. There are no sharp differences in the facets of the love experience treated by the poems, and although it is possible to define general emphases, the kinship of intent linking them together is the poet's passion. Therefore, the concepts that we underline are mere points of entry, not at all a classification.

In the first composition, "Salvador," the lover finds that all options in his life belong to the will of the loved one:

> Save him or damn him
> For now his destiny
> Is in your hands, abolished.
>
> If you are savior, save him
> From you and him; the violence
> Of not being one in you, allay it.
>
> Or if you are not, damn him,
> So that to his desire
> May succeed another torment.
>
> Save him or damn him,
> But do not let him thus
> Continue to live and lose you.

The lover is faced with a *fait accompli* that precludes in him even the decision to surrender his destiny, a situation aptly reflected by the reference to himself as "he," a being of diminished selfhood, a possession. It will be up to the beloved to decide; the alternatives presented are trenchant and almost impose the choice: "Save him or damn him" (*RD*, 304). Herein penetrates the sophistry of love, for the situation thrust upon the beloved by the lover limits the former's possibility of choice, and the middle alternative between condemning and saving does in fact exist: it is another way of condemning. What the lover has done is to *demand* a response from the beloved, some action on his part, an inescapable decision, thereby awakening him to the presence and plight of love. There is a further restriction in the loved one's power to choose in that the name given him predisposes his nature to the first alternative in two ways: first, as the creator, in language, of his presence, the namer invests him with the responsibility born of the name; second, because the entire poem is a development of the metaphorical potential contained within the name. The options have then become one, salvation, since ultimately the mere recognition of love in the lover by the beloved is salvation from indifference. There has been a curtailment of available choices, but also a parallel curtailment of expectations so that coincidence may ensue.

Poem III, "Para tí, para nadie" ("For You, For No One"), involves another use of language toward the framing of love's conditions where the backward glance acquires a particularly eloquent connotation; it is here, rather than in the previous instance, that we witness the poet's actual surrender of himself to the possible union with his beloved. The poem reveals his need for a last glimpse of the friend while there is yet time:

> Since memory is not enough
> When there is still time
>
> Someone who moves away
> Turns back his head
>
> Or that one who has already left
> In something possessive
>
> A letter, a picture
> The material traits
>
> Seeks, the faithful presence
> With earthly reality.
>
> And I, this Luis Cernuda,
> Unknown, who lasts

> A mere brief space
> Of hopeful love
>
> Before ending my term
> Of life, to your image,
>
> So beloved I turn
> Here, in thought,
>
> And although you will not see them
> To speak with your absence
>
> I write these lines,
> Solely to be with you.

(RD, 305–6)

At the center of the poem stands the man, Luis Cernuda. He has submitted to the creation of this meeting with those words that name him and contain all of him as both a living person and a writer. For there is a sense in which this composition may be viewed as the "birth of a poem." We have first a look that gives an image; then an image that elicits a memory, finally, a remembrance, with an image and a thought, sources of the poetic elaboration.

Only the poem can shape anew the coveted togetherness, for it contains previous, insufficient attempts and makes them a part of its own development. To suggest the greater stability of the event that originates in poetry rather than mere looking or remembrance, there has been a gradual increase in the containing power of each one of the three activities; the first, looking, while more immediate is least lasting—"Someone," the subject, finds its verb in the very next line "turns." The second activity, remembering, has expanded already: there are three lines between "That one" and "seeks" while the image has multiplied; the third, creating, reaches to the maximum limits: the last half of the poem belongs to it, and it contains the image sought and its maker as well as an interchange of actions between both. The first line of this development—"And I, this Luis Cernuda"—is echoed by the last which also completes it syntactically, closing the circle of creation. Here, Luis Cernuda, poet and lover, is a necessary element in a poem that expresses the essence of his being as a creative artist by displaying its own birth; at the same time, this actual appearance in the composition endows the image of the beloved also with greater existential substance to bring about the union.

"For You, For No One" is a highly representative instance of the "lover as creator" concept, one of the principal themes variously developed by most of the "Poems for a Body." This idea of love is clearly admitted in Poem IV, "Shadow of Myself," where the loved one is but ". . . the shadow/Of love which exists in me," an occasion for love to pour forth; but we know how essential love is for Cernuda, as a man and as a poet, and by the end of the poem the pretext has become the aim and purpose of his whole existence: "For this I came into the world, to await you;/To live because of you, as you live/ Because of me, even though you do not know it, / Because of this deep love I have for you"[5] (*PC*, 149). Poem VIII reiterates the theme of the beloved as a reason not merely for love, but for life. The concept, however, is developed in a direction opposite to that of Poem IV, for the poem begins with strong affirmations on the arrival of love as the crowning of existence. After insisting on the indispensability of the beloved's presence, the conclusion admits: "The odd thing is that at the same time/I know that you do not exist/Outside of my thought" (*RD*, 309–10). Poem IX also explores this idea and could be read as an expansion of the lines just quoted. The poet can scarcely imagine that the object of his passion should have parents, brothers, a family, so much a part of his thought, of his existence does he seem to be: ". . . your existing . . ./. . . seems to me unique/Created by my love . . ./A pure knowing gave you life" (*RD*, 310).

The answer to "Pastime," that short composition in which the arrival of love was the only possible redemption of the poet's multiple losses, is given by Poem X. His life is here recomposed in its fullness by a being whose presence contains all the vanished elements of his previous existence: homeland, people, life itself:

> My country?
> You are my country.
>
> My people?
> You are my people.
>
> Exile and death
> For me are where
> You are not.
>
> And my life?
> Tell me, my life,
> What is it, if not you?

$\qquad\qquad\qquad\qquad\qquad\qquad\qquad\qquad\qquad$ (*PC*, 153)

In Poem XII the beloved brings life, like the sun, but the life he brings is finite, and darkness will rise for night must come. The attunement achieved in this love experience is an inner one. It is a coincidence of desire and its object at the existential level, since the object is another human being and not the higher harmony. That is why the "Fín de la apariencia" ("End of Appearance") referred to in the title of Poem XIII involves a new awareness of things as seen from the heart of their contingency. The lover is cast adrift from the material world, his life bound to the only remaining inner necessity, "the task of loving":

> Dying seems easy,
> It is life that is difficult:
> I no longer know whether to use it
> In you, with this useless
> Task of loving you
> Which you do not heed.
>
>   (*RD*, 313)

While the realization of temporality continues to obtain in these love poems, the poet's attitude toward it has undergone a change of direction, in that duration is now to be plumbed fully rather than transcended. Because desire has found an object that absorbs it within reality, only in the present will desire find its fulfillment; for like all things material, that object is prone to decay. As Poem VII suggests, the full force of passion may make itself felt even at this late date; it should aim to do so in the completeness of the instant, ignorant of external limits to its manifestation. This is the lesson that the lover must now learn. It is a difficult lesson as it involves a reversal of emphasis in the constituent of reality that desire has forever struggled against: time. The didactic "you" address is returned to in this lyric: the lover is told to learn from nature itself the ability to ignore the pressures of time:

> . . . Were ever fruit
> Or perfume out of season,
> Or a bird on the wing?
>
> Break down the doors of time,
> Oh love who calls so late.
>
>   (*PC*, 151)

Poem XI, "El amante divaga" ("The Lover Rambles"), is a musing on the possibilities of expanding the duration of the privileged moment of love and concludes with the acceptance of worldly—and thus limited—experience as all we are ever likely to enjoy. The lover wonders about the structure of time in hell and seems provisionally to suppose that time flows backward. Should that be the case, he would relive the love story from oblivion through its peak to the preceding time of unawareness:

> But in hell, in that way,
> I would cease to believe, and at the same time
> The idea of paradise I would reject;
> Hell and paradise,
> Could they not be our own affair, from this
> Earthly life to which we are used and that is enough?
>
> (RD, 311–12)

Besides implying that heaven and hell are an invention of the moment of love and depend upon it for their existence, the poem underlines the extreme elusiveness of this moment caught between ignorance and oblivion as between heaven and hell. And yet, out of this minute of existence, both eternities are born. Poem XV expresses a similar idea; it sees in love the only condition whereby the lover, mere created being—"A body subject to time"—perceives eternity and elicits God's jealousy:

> For the time of love is worth to us
> A whole eternity
> Where man no longer goes alone,
> And God is jealous.

This is as close as "Poems for a Body" comes to the mystical concept of love; although there is some transcendence of time, it is more a matter of emotional equivalence between the love instant and eternity, not an overcoming of the temporal as was sought and expressed in those poems dealing with cosmic harmony. Still, the value of these moments is great enough for the deity to be jealous and to oversee their end:

> . . . One day
> Soon or late, God
> Sees to it that the lover should
> Renounce his love.
>
> (RD, 315)

While love retains its significance as a life force, the impetus of creation, it does so in these poems at the level of concrete existence. Cernuda gains an intense awareness of himself and finds himself entire in his experience. He is temporarily reconciled with reality or its image through a lover's eyes, and if the anguish of decay and change remains, it leads him not to a denial of the ephemeral but to its exaltation. This sequence of meditations on love provide a fitting counterpart to the first half of *With Time Running Out,* for they answer many of its somber queries and seem to infuse fresh energy and provide another source of inspiration to Cernuda's poetry. In this total subordination of the self to the love experience as to an ethical imperative, Cernuda has attained one of his clearest moments of self-apprehension not through rejection but involvement. For an instant reality and desire meet and coincide.

CHAPTER 7

The Disconsolate Chimera

*D*esolación de la quimera (The Disconsolate Chimera),[1] although dated 1956–1962, was written for the most part in the last year and a half of Cernuda's life, between the summer of 1960 and February, 1962, the date of composition of his final poem "A sus paisanos" ("To His Countrymen").[2] Between 1956, when *With Time Running Out* was completed and 1960, he wrote no poetry, according to his friend C. P. Otero, only returning to it in California where he was visiting assistant professor at the University of California at Los Angeles. It was in 1960 also that he learned of the death of his two sisters and felt himself in death's shadow. Harris believes that this circumstance may also have been instrumental in his resumption of writing: "[the] . . . presentiment that he was soon to die . . . turns this book into a poetic last will and testament designed to leave behind him an accurate self-portrait and a duly notarized statement of his account with life."[3]

It is easy to read too much of Cernuda's life into his work, especially since he developed himself at length the relationship between both, though always in quite general terms. The material we must work with, however, remains centrally the poetry, and we should be careful to let the voice speak untrammeled. In this sense we see that there have been no changes of direction in *The Disconsolate Chimera* although some shift of emphasis is noticeable. Still important, the exploration of love is resumed on a general plane with respect to previously pondered constants: love recreating reality, narcissism—and its corollary, homosexual passion—and the chasm between the beloved and the lover; and it is resumed on an individual plane with respect to the resistance of desire to aging as well as the personal memory of a past love affair. The problem of Spain also reappears, Cernuda's attitude to his homeland remaining bitterly accusatory for the most part. Aesthetic creation and poetry itself are dealt with in a number of poems in which the dominant theme remains the idea of art restructuring a chaotic world.

There is also in this collection a sprinkling of *poèmes de circonstance* (circumstantial or historically inspired poems) celebrating past friendships, evoking pleasant settings, attacking enemies. The frequency of these compositions indicates new attention to things more mundane, as if Cernuda were setting his house in order, taking care of last details in anticipation of his final days. Whereas in *Living Without Being Alive*, in the section preceding "Poems for a Body," the "settling of accounts" was of a spiritual nature, that of *The Disconsolate Chimera* concerns the baggage of daily life. In some of these pieces the man has often the best of the poet and the results are uneven.

I *Love's Traces*

Cernuda's preoccupation with love continues after the climax of "Poems for a Body," if not with comparable intensity, certainly as a major theme. Even those poems, written in a period of erotic immediacy, harbored the growth of a mental rather than physical passion; they presented us with the apparent paradox of a poet who, tracing the source of his inspiration to a core of sexual desire, turns his gaze inward to contemplate a largely intellectual adventure. But there is of course no contradiction in this; the object of love *is* a creation of our desire and does not exist truly as we see it. Cernuda's reflection surrounds this wellspring of metaphor, and in *The Disconsolate Chimera* love is pondered through the condition of the spirit at its margin, looking back or anticipating. Also, in the most important poem of the collection, "Luis de Bavaria escucha 'Lohengrin' " ("Ludwig of Bavaria Listens to 'Lohengrin' "), love is the source of a reborn, unshackled inner life.

In "Pregunta vieja, vieja respuesta" ("Old Question, Old Answer") departed love bequeaths but lingering lust, hiding a void. There is here an echo of Poem XII from *Where Oblivion Dwells* ("It is not love that dies, it is ourselves"), but whereas in the earlier poem love was the substance of life, now man simply becomes somebody else, as if his aging were a series of deaths, each one that of a different aspect of himself. Thus the "question" about love is answered later, but by another "persona" of the poet: "Where does love go when it is forgotten?/It is not he to whom you asked the question/Who answers you today." Already in this first stanza the poet's being is divided into three voices: first, the addressed "you," who remains throughout the poem as interlocutor; second, the self questioned in the past; third, the self who answers now. This last personification is the speaker in the poem, presumably the "present" man. The pendular movement through time characteristic of the rest of the poem is also anticipated in these opening lines: there is a rapid shift from past to present in which the question as well as the interlocutor remain the same.

The next stanza concerns the identity of the replier whose ability to answer is owed to longer years and time out of love employed in meditating on love's nature: he is the present man. The temporal sweep is repeated, since the distance from past to present is implied in the accumulation of years—" . . . a few more years of life/Gave him the occasion. . . ." Stanza three expands the time span by delving into the far past through a simile introducing the child's own world of desire, toys; at the same time, the inference that love seems now as a toy since like them it disappeared (stanza four), implies that the aspect of love about which the question is asked may not be its most essential one. The question is answered in part by strophe five: "The man who grows old, finds in his mind,/In his desire, empty, without charm,/Where loves go." Man's own transformations destroy the component of love tied to events, that is, to specific love objects, while retaining of it the form, desire. Stanza six completes the answer: lust remains as a husk of that part of passion which found transient fulfillment outside of itself. The poem concludes with a repetition of the first stanza now containing the response in another form: love disappears through the interstices of the divided self.

The past to present arc of the temporal pendulum has remained explicitly or by implication in each strophe. Along this sweep of time are recalled the several past instances of the present man—a dispersion lasting to the end and the reason for love's intermittences. The love here considered vanishes because it proves unequal to the task of overcoming the sundering of the self through time. It was part of reality, and like it, discontinuous.

And yet there was fulfillment in that great moment of love retraced by "Poems for a Body." As we noticed, the concept of cosmic yearning was absent, the lover entirely taken by desire for the immediate, by the exhausting of the present—a condition reminiscent of the "Garden" metaphor. In retrospect, where solitude calls forth a higher urgency, past erotic experience, complete though it was, becomes comparable to late afternoon in a walled garden, a transient bliss menaced by night. Still, the affair of "Poems for a Body," a moment of greatest abandon, is recalled with fondness now in "Epílogo" ("Epilogue") where Cernuda admits the temptation to deny ultimate value to the event but finally resists it.

The poem takes its points of departure from a photograph, a square of paper holding fast the cherished image with its material and temporal coordinates:

> Beach of "la Roqueta":
> On the stone, against the cloud,
> Amid the air you are, with me
> Who invisible breathe love around you.
> Yet you are not you, but your image.
>
> Your image of years ago
> Beautiful as always, on the paper. . . .

The words of the poem—it *is* an "afterword"—will proceed to liberate this picture by giving it, though also on paper, new life and meaning: it will be as an expansion of the "breath" of love (line four). Quickly, the distance in time and space is bridged, for in the mind there is yet another image of the past beloved and of that time past which may bring solace once more. Thoughts of that instant's ephemerality prompt doubts about its true value: " . . . why all that:/The torment of loving, ancient as the world,/That a few instants manage to recover?/Love's labors lost." But at all costs value must not be denied the event, for it would be denying value to life itself:

> In the hour of death
> (If man can make predictions for it, calculations),
> Your image at my side
> Will perhaps smile at me as it smiled at me today,
> Illuminating this existing dark and remote
> With love, only light of the world.
>
> (*RD*, 360–61)

Though merely remembered, love has given the photograph—appearance merged with its occasion—temporal, emotional, and ethical substance, while transforming physical into aesthetic beauty. It is now wholly a creation of the mind and belongs to lasting desire, "only light of the world."

Such infrequent instances of idealization are like bright flashes in the night of love's recollection where anguish and madness remain. The poet is now reluctant to respond when love again solicits him:

> Venom and antidote together is
> The ancient insidious enchantment:
> In the body created by your love
> You still hope to nourish your eyes.
>
> (*RD*, 362–63)

This final strophe of "Love Still" summarizes in two striking, parallel metaphors some of the principal components of late Cernudian love: (1) It is a danger and a salvation at the same time, for it implies the surrender of oneself and probably suffering,[4] since it will merely exacerbate desire, both physical and mental. (2) The beloved is created by the poet-lover in that his image does not correspond to reality; he is spiritually renewed, since by recreating him, the lover abstracts a part of the beloved from the decay of time. (3) Narcissistic overtones are once more present, since in the lover's creation there enters such a large portion of himself, that it is actually a gaze upon another form of his own self. Sight, as we have seen, is also the source of both intellectual and mystical speculation because it captures light, the Apollonian Platonic principle.

The great poem "Ludwig of Bavaria Listens to 'Lohengrin' " contains, under the predominance of narcissism, forms of those three components of love, supported by the most essential element of all in Cernuda's amatory system: flight from this world appears the one available alternative but finally proves both impossible and insufficient. The work's structure rests on a series of dualities ranging from the most apparent, opposing Ludwig's inner and outer worlds, to the most intimate in which he dreams of another image of himself. These disjunctions remain ultimately unresolved.

The opening is dominated by imagery of music as water with the stage a poollike cavern.[5] Ludwig, for whose sole pleasure the performance of Wagner's "Lohengrin" is given, looks upon the magic cavern transfixed: "His half-closed eyes listen, drinking in the melody / As thirsting land absorbs the gift of water." On a background of growing dichotomies—retreat from the outside world into that of the theater, actual and mental distance to the stage—Ludwig's imagination attempts a first merging:

> He sees a double performance; one outside, the one
> He is attending; the other within, there in his mind,

> Where both combine (as form and color combine
> Together in a body) and become one delight.

The power which has allowed him to create the dreamworld he is now contemplating also helped him to build its semblance outside, to live in near freedom a species of legend: "His place is on his kingdom's highest snowy peaks." And yet this power vanished when he met youth and beauty, becoming its slave. Also, therefore, the disjunction remained.

The second moment of inner recognition begins in stanza seven: "Floating on the music the dream is now made flesh:/A white, blond, beautiful youth, who stands/Beside him, and is himself. . . ." From the pool of music onstage in a magical cavern, like Narcissus, Ludwig sees his double rise to meet him; the king finds himself in the mythical youth and is seduced. His dream turns the legendary hero into his own mirror image. And yet, as for Narcissus, this love can find no consummation; the thirst will remain unslaked and the question unanswered: "Is it not enough that what he loves exists outside him?/Is not the contemplation of beauty sufficient recompense?" The union, begun as the spectacle on the stage and the spectacle in the mind echoed one another, is completed and the fulfillment of desire that dreams can offer is attained, though in alienation, in the limbo of exiled gods:

> Fused with the myth he watches, already part
> of that myth
> Of rebel purity, hardly touching the earth,
> The ether's exiled guest. The melody helps
> him to know himself,
> To love his real self, and in the music he
> lives forever.

But even in his ultimate retreat to insanity, Ludwig finds the distance between desire and its object unbridged: ". . . the king's destiny,/To desire himself, transforms him into something/As beautiful, vulnerable, and useless as a flower" (*PC*, 156–63). The anguish of perpetually seeing the beloved outside himself, although in his own image, repeats in his dream world the pattern of reality he escaped from. The essential separation of the worlds within and without, ingredient as a basic pattern in the poem, leaves intact the distance between reality and desire. The surpassing of time and decay afforded by the higher consonance adumbrated and sometimes achieved in earlier poems is absent here because desire has limited its scope; whatever fulfillment it may attain, it will be contained by its object.

II   *This World's Beauty*

For Cernuda the beauty of this world resides in its re-creation by art; in the coherence that aesthetic form gives to the dispersion of objects and events, material and spiritual. Many of the poems in *The Disconsolate Chimera* are devoted to the conditions of this activity in the poet and other artists.

The first poem in the collection, "Mozart 1756–1956," is a tribute to the great composer on the bicentenary of his birth. It follows the pattern of Cernuda's meditative poetry, in this instance from the musician's individual history to the human significance of his work. It is divided into three parts of three stanzas each, the first concerning Mozart—the man and the artist; the second, his music; and the third, its worth to humanity. As an undertone in the first three and the last three strophes, but absent in the central section, the contrast between the lasting but invisible power of the composer's creation and the visible but ephemeral influence of circumstance highlights the ultimate triumph of art over the accidents of history.

The opening stanza presents Mozart as the incarnation of music, and music itself in metaphors of water and vitality that stress the art's generative impulse: ". . . we hear its whispering lymphlike pace, / With the coolness given by moons and dawns, / Growing into cascades, into copious rivers." After tracing the course of the musical "spirit" as part of Western civilization's inheritance from Greece, Mozart is set at the apex of Europe's creative impetus, the true echo of that classical tradition. He entertained "princes and prelates" who knew his genius only when he died. The representatives of worldly might are both lay and religious; the form they give to society is merely appearance, and their action incidental when compared to the coherency represented by musical invention. It is to this coherency that the central part of the poem turns. Its three stanzas evoke the power of Mozart's music as to form, content, and inspiration, respectively, in imagery of flight, sculpting water, and erotic desire.

The last three strophes exalt the value of the composer's music for man in his impotence. It liberates him from social and political subservience, from the smothering weight of habit and profitless labor, by opening his mind to its potential nobility: ". . . man can still / Let his humiliated mind be ennobled / With the peerless harmony. . . ." It gives continuity to the disconnected elements of reality; God's formless and unjust creation is restructured by music:

> . . . from God's hands formless came the world forth
> Its order overturned, terrible its unjustice;
> . . . .
> This music gives form to the world, order, justice,
> Nobility and beauty. . . .

There is no need for bloody crucifixions, no sin to be redeemed by sacrifice. Music rescues man from life by returning to him a parcel of divinity, reawakening the image of his true forgotten self, the lasting essence that owes obeisance to no gods: "Yes, man passes, but his voice lasts long, / Nocturnal nightingale or morning lark, / Ringing in the ruins of heaven and the gods" (*RD*, 319–21).

For Cernuda, Mozart's harmonies are echoes of the music moving the world, and the composer is supreme among those artists who can be intermediaries of man to that higher realm—all creators of beauty are actually transmitters of beauty to a greater or lesser degree though this capacity is in constant danger; we saw, for instance, that in "The Tree," from *Living Without Being Alive,* the gift is lost. Cernuda believes that the potential to discover one's lasting essence exists in all of us and has nothing to do with original sin or any other kind of religious arbitration. In fact, his concept of God recalls here the Gnostic demiurge, evil creator of the material world, of the veil hiding the superior sphere of reality from us. The mystical note on which the poem ends effectively transforms Mozart into a true intercessor, an aspect of the traditional Sophia or Guide, illuminator of the mind of man, who can free us from the darkness of matter. We must keep in mind that for Cernuda the artist does not represent what he sees around him but recomposes it. In that sense beauty exists not in reality but in its artistic reincarnation, for the real is of itself inert. That is why in "Dostoievsky y la hermosura física" ("Dostoyevsky and Physical Beauty") the writer is equally to be praised for seeing or inventing the youth Falalei's physical beauty:

> Dostoyevsky can no longer tell us
> Whether he invented Falalei or found him in life,
> Whether he invented beauty or knew to see it.
> . . . .
> But the merit is equal in both cases.

(*RD*, 322)

Ultimately, the recognition of such beauty springs from desire, as does its creation, so that the difference between both activities vanishes. Dostoyevsky's fortitude is opposed to Goethe's possible fear of describing male beauty and grows out of the wish to present a moral rather than a physical portrait: "Representing physical beauty/He left us an image of moral beauty." But here, too, the contrast is merely apparent, for both forms of beauty originate in love. Passion at the source gave Dostoyevsky the will to see and draw such form; perhaps it was wanting in "old Goethe."

The weight of years need not burden the core of desire. We have seen how Cernuda's susceptibility to passion remained to the end, how he retained his deep love for the potential beauty of the human form—potential in that it truly blooms only under the lover's gaze. In "Ninfa y pastor, por Ticiano" ("Nymph and Shepherd by Titian") he chooses a painting done by the Venetian master near his hundredth year to illustrate the indestructibility of love in the great artist, a love that had opted early for things human and kept unswervingly to this decision. And it becomes abundantly clear not only that the painting is a mirror for the painter's always young fervor, but that the painter's fervor is a mirror to the poet's, also still young.

The poem begins with (on first impression) a candid admission of preference of things human, contrasting the saint's "superhuman" gaze heavenward and his renunciation of earthly things to the poet's—and the painter's—own, level with things:

> That which moves the saint,
> The saint's renunciation
> (Deny your desires
> And you will then find
> What your heart desires)
> Are superhuman. There you bow and you pass.
> Because some were born to be saints
> And others to be men.

But soon we discover that the artist's creation and his embrace of the world to this purpose realize in him a full humanity before which the saint's renunciation appears thin and bloodless. The piece becomes a strong statement of self-assertion by the poet in continuing concurrence with his past.

This note is immediately struck in the second stanza which introduces also the true subject of the poem in the poet himself, brother of the Renaissance artist:

> Perhaps close to leaving life,
> Repenting nothing and still in love,
> And with a passion that gives not the lie to the
>   first one,
> You would want, like the old painter,
> Once more to represent the human form,
> Silently speaking with a science now admirable.

It is significant that Cernuda should choose a previous work of art as the basis for his own representation of "human form." Again, it is not the raw world of existence to which he is attentive, unless such existence is liable to artistic recomposition. In this case there is no contact whatsoever with this world: "You still look at that painting, / Now not in its reality, in memory." The gaze is turned inward to the memory of a painting, itself the recreation of a myth. We have thus a multiplied artificiality; the poet returns to language, the plastic form of a previous linguistic structure. And yet the sensuousness of the scene remains intact, even enhanced, as the tactile work of the painter is magnified by repetition to become the tactile work of the poet:

> The creating imprint still fresh in it,
> The imprint of the loving fingers
> Which, under their caress, animated it
> With animal candor and with earthly grace.

Titian's loving gesture reverberates through the poem, captured in the poet's echoing delight. The form born of his fingers bears witness to the lasting vigor of his sensual and artistic desire:

> Close to a prodigious hundred years
> But his human fervor, grateful to the world,
> Was still innocent in him, as in the lad
> Destined to be man alone and forever.

> (*RD*, 326–27)

The very activity of the artist supersedes the object being created as loving does its own object. Finally, the recall of the first stanza in the last one offers this creative communion as a richer alternative than is the "saint's" sterile communion with absence.

III   *The Poet in Solitude*

Few artists enjoyed as long and serene an existence as Titian; even he was forced to depend on the whim of patrons. The ordeal and privilege of the artist's condition has remained for Cernuda a compelling paradox, appearing almost invariably as a component of his poems on the poet's disposition. Solitude, we know, is almost inevitable to the *poète voyant* ("seer") to use Rimbaud's term, and perhaps a necessary state for the reception of the gift. In the poem "Niño tras un cristal" ("Child Behind a Windowpane"), this state is the beautiful affliction producing a pearl. In his room the child watches the falling rain through a window. From the glistening world outside we penetrate to an enveloping, solitary warmth inside, then within the child to the realm of imagination, reaching finally the generative center: "He lives in the bosom of his tender strength/ . . ./In his shadow the pearl is already forming" (*RD*, 321–22). This poem is a final reverbation of several of Cernuda's earliest pieces concerning the birth of poetry in solitude and also of "The Family," where the child's "difference," his rejection of customary values, is an alienness growing in the darkness within him. Remarkable in its consistency from the beginning, Cernuda's interpretation of his poetic impulse is never free of some destructive characteristics. The poet's charge implies the forsaking of much that may be joyful, for the gain of some portion of knowledge. The decision went without saying, for only the wily pragmatist resists the sirens' song.

In "Las sirenas" ("The Sirens") the opening stanza defines the conditions in which the sirens' song may still be heard, some unchanged, some new. Unchanged is our ignorance of their language; unchanged also is their chant, "That very song which Ulysses resisted." But the sirens themselves have been tamed, so to speak, and their terrors mitigated. They are not out at sea but inland in some lake perhaps, where their enchantment need not be deadly. And yet, while now those who hear it can return, the song still casts a spell:

> . . . but the song remained
> Philter, potion of tears, imbibed into their spirit,
> And they felt within with deep resonance
> The enchantment in the chant of the aging siren.

We may not understand this plaint, but our spirit thirsts for it. Our innermost being has not changed though even an elderly siren now holds sufficient charm to capture it. Those prudent as Ulysses or even merely indifferent, deaf to those accents, resist with ease. Those passionate go to meet it and are marked forever: "Can one single song thus change a life?/The chant had ceased, the sirens fallen silent, and their echoes./He who listens to them once remains widowed and desolate forever" (*RD*, 323). The poet's devotion to the sirens' song has claimed his entire being. His life's work has been an effort to reproduce that melody from another, forgotten realm of existence and as always, at the core of his undertaking was a decision of passion.

A similar metaphor of capture or bewitchment inspires "The Disconsolate Chimera," the poem from which the collection takes its title. The premise of the fallen deity which it also explores recalls such earlier compositions as "Undertow in Sansueña," "The Ages," and "To the Gods' Statues." The statue of the chimera lies mutilated and corroded in an ossuary. The mythical being has fallen. Moon and stars look down from the highest firmament in contempt, but the moonlight awakens some ghostly life in the broken stone: ". . . The Chimera whispers at the moon/And her voice is so sweet that it relieves the desolation." Alone in the barren land, forgotten as the bones that surround her, the beast longs for death. Although the gods have disappeared, divinity remains and has left in her the ancient yearning to see man's beauty enslaved. But all men now disdain her secrets save for poets: "Poets, I find no charm in them,/Since my secret scarcely tempts them, nor do I see beauty in them." Even they have almost forgotten her, as well they might, given their own condition: "Can they believe in being poets/If they no longer have the power, the madness/To believe in me and in my secret?" (*RD*, 350–53). The Chimera's divine madness returns the faintest pulse from some few of these men. The poet of today finds the mistress that he deserves. As in "The Sirens," Cernuda sees a mutual downfall in the poet and his myths, although both must continue their dialogue until the end.

Cernuda attributes the decay of poetic intensity to the almost insurmountable pressures of bourgeois society and of academicized art. Writers strong enough to withstand it during their lifetime are sure to have their work reinterpreted and domesticated after death. He felt such pressures himself throughout his career, exacted mainly as unavoidable economic necessities, and fought hard against them. His homosexuality also isolated him, of course, and we see through his poetry that he neither tried to veil it, nor did he emphasize it unduly. As an essential aspect of himself and linked to the erotic song of his inspiration, it is also an integral part of his poetry. It belongs also to his self-assertive struggle for completeness which he wants neither forgotten nor offhandedly dismissed. His fear is that, as for Rimbaud and Verlaine in "Birds in the Night," society needs to transform to its own image those comfortably dead:

> Today, since time has passed, as in the world
>   happens,
> Life at the margin of all, sodomy, drunkenness,
>   scornful verse,
> No longer matter in them, and France makes use
>   of both names and the works of both,
> For the greater glory of France and its logical art.

Verlaine was quick to return to the fold, and even the rebellious Rimbaud at the end "drags in his belt the gold he has won" (*RD*, 324–26). Such are the contrasts of the poet's life. Rimbaud was sustained in his revolt by the very poetry he wrote. Having later chosen silence, ancestral characteristics won him over. Verlaine's poetry was invigorated and transformed by his stormy friendship with Rimbaud; having chosen loquaciousness, his verse became tame.

The condition of the poet among men gains renewed importance in *The Disconsolate Chimera* at a time when man and poet, never truly separated in Cernuda, must stand even closer together awaiting the end. It is time to see whether the man's experience and the poet's intuition can merge, and so he has looked around him to other men and other poets to learn again about living. Yet, what he sees is still contradiction. In "El poeta y la bestia" ("The Poet and the Beast"), after recalling how Goethe's life was endangered by drunken soldiers of Napoleon quartered in his home, how close we were to losing the second and perhaps greatest part of his work, Cernuda wonders at the great poet's lasting admiration of the French emperor: "It is paradoxical that, in spite of everything, Goethe should admire / Napoleon, and that he should continue to admire him for the rest of his days" (*RD*, 343–45).

The birth of the poem, the potential for form in nature and youth, continue to represent for him havens of calm enjoyment. In "Tres misterios gozosos" ("Three Joyful Mysteries") early day, early childhood, and the unfinished poem all contain the same joy.[6] In its nascent state the poem may contain the birth of light and song, with dawn—"The singing of the birds, at dawn / When the day is mildest"; the happiness and innocence of childhood—". . . the little child plays alone/By himself and in happy/Ignorance enjoys being alive"; the poet's dream:

> The poet, dreaming upon the paper,
> His unfinished poem,
> Finds it beautiful, rejoices and thinks
> With good reason and madness
> That nothing matters, his poem exists.
>
> (*RD*, 353–54)

Close to sixty, Cernuda still saw in poetry a science of beginnings. The poem seems here not a means of reaching the overarching harmony or an expression of the distance between things and between men, but the moment that precedes disjunction.

IV *Spain: The Final Glance*

As for his own return to the beginning, that voyage home taken by some of the writers exiled since the Civil War, Cernuda feels no temptation. He despises Franco's Spain as a dead land for dead people: " . . . your country, the country of the dead, / Where everything now is born dead, / Lives dead and dies dead." These lines in "Díptico Español, I, Es lástima que fuera mi tierra" ("Spanish Diptych, I, It is a Pity that It was my Country") sum up the unabated bitterness he feels still when considering his homeland's present state. But we would have an incomplete picture of the poet's relationship to his homeland were we not to read both parts of "Spanish Diptych." We know from other poems on Spain's past, those on Philip II, that aspects of it did represent some things of value for him and that, while he may feel that the country's present condition is no mere accident, the seeds of such decay were there already, he also knows that it possessed as well in its people the potential for positive transformation. The two poems that compose the "Diptych" express both views.

In Poem I Cernuda begins by setting in what he believes to be the proper perspective the role played by Spain in his own work, calling it *one* of his voices. He then expands on that aspect of his Spanish inheritance to which he feels tied: the gains made by man's spirit. And what he rejects is to see these gains denied and the denial tolerated. Only death remains under such conditions: ". . . ponderous procession / With restored relics and remains, / To which give escort vestments and uniforms." Soldiers and clerics lead the silent march, the soldiers of today, representing the culmination of Spain's warrior tradition and its enmity to life; today's clerics, also the culmination of the fanatic tradition that condemned reason, calling it pride. (Both archaisms join in the shout "Death to intelligence," uttered with impunity.)[7]

The language, poetry, remains an unbreakable bond with the land, but it belongs to the people and their roots; through it they are liberated. It is to those who continue to respect life and reason that the poet addresses himself:

> . . . I speak by myself
> . . . .
> Or for those few who may listen to me
> With well disposed understanding.
> Those, who like me, respect
> Human free will.

This link to Spain continues strong, the true inheritance Cernuda claims. The rejection of Spain is a rejection of what Spain has become which for him represents a flourishing of its worst characteristics, but he maintains at the same time that such is not its essence. In this sense, it is possible to include this denial of the homeland in the broader spectrum of his poetic concerns where, as he says, are many voices: "Where the one thought dominant/Is merely one voice among the others."

Cernuda explores an unrealized picture of Spain in "Díptico II, Bien está que fuera tu tierra" ("Diptych II, It is Fortunate that It Was Your Country"). From the opening lines we enter into the realm of imagination, the meeting ground of mind and books, where reality and desire may agree. Literature has already given form to the discontinuity of events, and man appears therein proportioned to his history; in his father's library, the child discovers the works of Galdós: "And you crossed the threshold of a magical world, / The other reality that is behind this one."

Recalled with particular fondness is the figure of Salvador Monsalud,[8] fighter for freedom and against tradition, and appropriate answer to those who in the previous poem took and imposed opposite standpoints. Also remembered with fondness are lesser characters of the novels, calm daily lives, hopeful and suffering people: those liberated by the poet's voice, whose language is theirs too. In this fictional context, more real than the actual one, names and landscapes acquire a substance lost to lived memory:

> The real one for you is not that depressing and
> obscene Spain

> In which today the rabble rules,
> Rather this Spain alive and always noble
> Which Galdós has created in his books.
> Of the former, the latter cures and consoles us.
>
> (RD, 328–34)

The backward steps taken by modern Spain toward a "sinister past" have denied their voice to all those who throughout its history sacrificed themselves against violence and unreason. Theirs is the voice that Cernuda wants to echo.

There is no thought of return for Cernuda because his own Spain stays with him, not merely a burden but also part of his liberation. Yet in some ways he was unable to gain complete freedom from bitter recollections. His last poem "A sus paisanos" ("To His Countrymen") is, in the guise of a farewell, a harsh invective against his compatriots who, he feels, rejected him from the beginning with their accustomed intolerance. It is astonishing to find in this final composition, alive and still painful, the memory of the reviews—not all bad by any means—of *Perfil del aire*. [9] Besides the attack on his first efforts, still unwarranted in his opinion, Cernuda's other point of contention is that the "legend"—"Doleful stories/Invented about me by four friends/(Friends?) . . ."—of his brittle, intractable, and difficult nature should have been so readily believed, another instance for the poet of his countrymen's congenital lack of reason. He regrets that he must use the same language and that the fate of his work should be in the hands of its speakers. And here he wants to separate himself from them still further for, he says, that tongue is merely "the material/I used in my writings . . ."; the personal idiom it became is his. The attack, though angry, is not indiscriminate. It singles out two very specific events—early criticism and myth—whose wounds have not yet healed. His entire life has been encumbered by these frustrations. The farewell is sincere in its anger—when it would have been easy to make peace—and also shrewd. He thanks those whose friendship he still values, but he feels unable to put on the cloak of sage forgiveness, "No more than you can placate that phantom you made of me" (PC, 166–71).

Spain as a creation of the spirit, independent of its present state, still beckons to Cernuda. In "1936," the penultimate poem of *The Disconsolate Chimera*, a veteran of the Lincoln Brigade calls forth anew in the poet the faith in the struggle that sustained so many during the Civil War and to which he subscribed himself, though not as a soldier; but beyond that, it is his faith in man that is rekindled:

> Remember it yourself and remember it to others,
> When disgusted by human baseness,
> When irate at human hardness:
> This man alone, this act alone, this faith alone.
> Remember it yourself and remember it to others.

This first stanza with its accented litanylike repetitions becomes an invocation, anchoring in the mind a crucial event whereby the faith displayed by the old soldier, a foreigner, becomes the faith regained by the native poet. Compared to present trivialities, those past events acquire new splendor; though the cause was lost, its essence, the trust that people had in it, has remained in this one man and is now renewed in the poet:

> Because of that today the cause seems to you
> As in those days:
> Noble and as worthy of fighting for it.
> And his faith, that faith, he maintained it.

It rises above the present and also its remote occasion, for it is sufficiently generous to encompass much more even now. One man's nobility can redeem the infamy of many: "One, only one is enough/ As the irrefutable witness/Of all human nobility" (*RD*, 364–65).

As always, Cernuda's acerbity, his disillusionment amid the welter and disparity of events, is mitigated by his persevering will to believe. This willingness to offer himself in his entirety with no reticence is one of his greatest strengths as a poet and combines with an equally forceful refusal to surrender any part of himself to expediency: "I only wanted to be/With my light and my love." ("Before Leaving"; *PC*, 154–55).

CHAPTER 8

Cernuda as Critic

C ERNUDA defined quite clearly the role he ascribed to his criticism in an interview with Fernández Figueroa, dated 1959: "Since I am, or fancy that I am a poet, criticism is for me but a marginal product of the poetic activity."[1] Although in this study we have turned to Cernuda's criticism only insofar as it highlighted important aspects of his poetry, the several books of critical commentary that he has left are of sufficient importance to merit close perusal themselves. At this point the limits of the present volume allow merely the barest delineation of this facet of the poet's work; we shall limit ourselves to a brief examination of *Estudios sobre poesía española contemporánea (Studies on Contemporary Spanish Poetry)* and some remarks on his other essays. It is hoped that a more thorough scrutiny of Cernuda's criticism may be undertaken in the near future, since his importance as a theorist in contemporary Spanish letters is steadily growing.

Cernuda's critical work consists principally of scattered articles or essays, collected in *Poetry and Literature I and II,* as well as the volume mentioned above on Spanish poetry and *Pensamiento poético en la lírica inglesa (siglo XIX) (Poetic Thought in English Lyricism [Nineteenth Century]).* A more recent collection of articles, *Crítica, ensayos y evocaciones (Criticism, Essays and Evocations)* appeared in 1970. This volume was edited and annotated by Luis Maristamy who, in happy disregard of Cernuda's wishes,[2] gathered together a number of important pieces from various newspapers and other sources written between 1929 and 1956. Circumstances compelled Cernuda to earn a living as both a journalist and a teacher. In this he ran true to a pattern of his generation remarkable for its poet-professors (Salinas and Guillén are other well-known examples), but he was probably the least affected of all by this role; always it remained wholly contingent to his essential self. He continued a poet in all his work, intuitive in

149

the initial evaluation of his subject, carefully controlled in his exposition.

Cernuda has never formally set forth a theory of poetry. The closest he has come to doing so, apart from those reflections on his own writing which are commented on in the body of this essay,[3] are the responses made in the interview with Figueroa. He there characterized a great poet (1) "by the melodic fusion in his verse of words, sense, and rhythm"; (2) "by the precision and beauty of his language"; (3) "by the amplitude of his vision"; and (4) "by the richness and flexibility of his thought."[4] While it is true that Cernuda stressed noticeably the poet's "voyance," or vision, close attention to form very early gained preeminence in his own verse. This equilibrium, which we encounter in most of his poems, is here also expressed in theoretical terms. For him, overemphasis in either aspect diminished poetic value, although he believed, like Eliot, that if a writer were to sin, it would be better to sin on the side of form. Nevertheless, he felt that the main defect of French poetry was its rhetoricism, a tendency he likewise criticized in the poetry of Spain. On the other hand, he was often also critical of unstructured lyrical outbursts; he found, for instance, that J. R. Jiménez overindulged in such flights of poetic fancy and censured him for it with growing acerbity.

Insofar as the evaluative component of his criticism is concerned, Cernuda prefers to allow his readers to arrive at it themselves and is content with assisting them in this task by stressing those aspects of the work in question which he considers relevant. He asserts in the interview with Figueroa: ". . . what as a critic I try to do . . . is to gather and expound the elements that I consider decisive in the work of the author discussed, leaving the matter of judging to the reader's responsibility. . . ."[5] Not infrequently, however, his judgments are either clearly manifested or easily deduced from his agreements or reservations on those two components of the poem which he always considered essential: forcefulness of vision and of expression.

We should not go to Cernuda for detailed exegesis of a text. His readings are generally straightforward elaborations of an initial intuition of the work's form followed by some commentary on its general import. His point of departure may be the work itself or it may just as frequently be the writer, for he eschews neither the historical nor the biographical background of his material. On the whole, he demonstrates a preference if not for intrinsic analysis as such, at least for intrinsic appreciation, since he considers at best hypothetical the links that may be discovered between an author and his work. In many instances, an overemphasis on the minutiae of erudition appears to him an impediment to the best understanding of a work of art. Of Cervantine scholarship he says: "So dense can be the mass of erudite commentaries accumulated on a work, that it becomes difficult to approach it . . . and we lose sight of it."[6] In the case of some poets with whom he felt great kinship, such as Hölderlin and Nerval, his understanding begins with that overwhelming empathy. These are among his most rewarding commentaries, for they are revealing of his own work as well as the brother poets'.

Of Cernuda's criticism *Studies on Contemporary Spanish Poetry* probably had the most immediate impact. Published in Spain, it elicited mixed—though on the whole not unfavorable—comments in spite of some unorthodox evaluations of past and present poets (as well as some telling reticences). After an introductory chapter on the failure of neoclassical and romantic writers to renovate Spanish poetry, while realizing the necessity of such renovation, Cernuda situates the first stirrings of new poetic thought in Campoamor: "Thus Campoamor, by introducing subjectivity in lyricism, takes a decisive step, discovering a path that neither the neoclassicals nor the romantics . . . could take."[7] Campoamor also realized that poetic language had to be reformed toward straightforwardness, and while his own efforts were unfortunately unequal to the task, he retains historical importance for having at least understood the direction in which lyricism had to move. Cernuda then takes a traditional position in anchoring contemporary poetry to the work of Bécquer: "After a strange lethargy of more than one and one half centuries, Spanish poetry awakens in the *Rimas* of Bécquer."[8] Bécquer's verse, of course, constituted Cernuda's own introduction to poetry, and this fellow Sevillian would occupy always a special place in his poetic world (see above, page 37). Beyond such personal preference Cernuda sees in Bécquer the counterpart of Garcilaso[9] in that both initiated a poetic tradition.

The generation of 1898 is introduced by a chapter on modernism. Here some customary assumptions are questioned. For one thing, Cernuda does not think that Darío was the sole originator of the movement. Salvador Rueda had been writing modernist verse when Darío arrived in Spain. Furthermore, modernism looked back to the late French romantics and to the Parnassians: ". . . it seems strange that the novelties imported to Spain by modernism should still be mentioned. Were not Lamartine, Hugo, Musset read to satiety by

our romantics?" (E, 66). Cernuda feels that the modernists stopped at
Symbolism and thereby disregarded the best French poetry of the
past century, that is, Nerval, Baudelaire, Rimbaud, and Mallarmé.[10]
As for the relationship between modernism and "el '98," while
Cernuda admits to certain mutual concerns such as aestheticism and a
desire for reform, he concludes that only in minor points was there a
recognizable, lasting influence by the American movement on
Spanish letters: "if modernism has some influence on us, it is only
with respect to the least important in contemporary poetry. . . .Its
contribution in themes, meters, vocabularies, has been rejected by
the new poetic generations, as a nourishment which the organism
neither digests nor assimilates" (E, 70).

From the Generation of 1898 Cernuda focusses on Unamuno,
Machado, and J. R. Jiménez. Despite his unmelodiousness and some
harshness of expression, Unamuno seems to him the greatest poet in
Spain in this century. He notes also that Unamuno's poetics goes
counter to that of modernism. For Cernuda, Unamuno is mostly a
poet, and because of this he fails as a philosopher; in his philosophical
work "intuition substitutes reason and the measured pace of reasoning is replaced by the sudden and intermittent advance of poetic
intuition" (E, 80). Machado also turns his back on modernism by
opting for the expression of a ". . . deep throbbing of the spirit"
(E, 85) rather than the sounds and sensations of Darío's verse.
Cernuda censures in Machado his belief in an "art of the people,"
which he feels is an invention of scholars and critics, but admires the
steadfastness of his adherence to the spiritual landscape of Spain
(translated politically into his equally steadfast anti-Fascist position)
and the "undeniable grandeur" (E, 90) with which he traced it. The
present preference for Machado's poetry by younger poets in contrast
to their distance from Jiménez, Cernuda attributes to their discovering in it still "some living echo to a certain anguish for 'the eternally
human' " (E, 94).

Juan Ramón Jiménez, while perhaps closer to modernism on the
surface than were Unamuno or Machado, actually favored the minor
symbolists such as Samain, Laforgue, Moréas, and also Verlaine.
Jiménez occupies a special place in Cernuda's criticism. His appreciation of the older poet's work changed drastically over the years from
early unbounded admiration to stringent criticism at the end. For
most of the members of the Generation of 1925, Jiménez was the poet
par excellence, and Cernuda, who as a young man was introduced to
him by Salinas, felt awed and speechless in his presence. Soon,

however, Jiménez's personality intruded upon Cernuda's appreciation of his verse to the extent that its reading became repugnant to
him. An article written in 1958 and included in *Poesía y Literatura*
speaks of the "two persons of Juan Ramón Jiménez" as a Jekyll-Hyde
case of split personality. Cernuda does not say whether his objectivity
suffered from this awareness, but he admits in any case that his
"youthful admiration for his work had gradually become extin-
guished, and there remained of it not the least ember" (*PL*, 291).
Jiménez's poetry was for him impressionistic and frequently devoid of
intellectual content. Neither its early superficiality nor its later forced
obscurity, he maintains, masked a continuing lack of composition.
Finally, he finds in Jiménez's latest poems lessened "poetic intensity
and vigor" (*E*, 105).

In a transitional position between the Generations of 1898 and 1925
are situated León Felipe, José Moreno Villa, and Ramón Gómez de la
Serna; the latter is included because of his great influence on the 1925
group, even though his work is in prose. For Cernuda, Gómez de la
Serna is an influence on poets of his own generation because he
represents a direct continuation of the great Spanish tradition of
"ingenio," becoming especially significant to those writers who
looked back to Góngora in 1927.

Cernuda appears somewhat reticent on the subject of his own
contemporaries and passes over in silence Aleixandre, Alberti, Diego, and Altolaguirre. The very few words he says on Guillén belong
to his section on Salinas, so that apart from a general introductory
chapter on the group only two poets are extensively examined:
Salinas and Lorca. In a prefatory note as well as in a footnote to his
Salinas chapter, Cernuda indicates that he chose to remain silent
when the poets happened to be personal friends or acquaintances,
and still living, for fear that his judgment might be less than objective.
What he does say of Guillén shows that he considered him a
"bourgeois" poet and did not like his work. As for Salinas, he finds
him overly precious. In contrast, his evaluation of Lorca is on the
whole cautiously generous; he believes that he may still have had his
best work ahead of him when he was killed.[11] As for the poets he
leaves aside, we know that his friendship with Aleixandre and
Altolaguirre lasted until the end and he has elsewhere expressed
admiration of the former and the opinion that the latter's poetry
deserved much closer study than it has heretofore received;[12] personal antagonisms undoubtedly colored his appreciation of Guillén's
poetry, while Alberti and Diego remain unknown quantities. The

book concludes with a short section on Miguel Hernández and younger poets. Of Hernández he says that although he was a born poet, he lacked craftsmanship. He finds some promise in recent Spanish poetry, although he thinks it is too early to form any judgment.

On the whole the book is well balanced and perceptive, especially on earlier writers. We must allow that a conflict of personalities blinded Cernuda to some of the values of his poetic generation. On the other hand, much of his severity is mitigated if we remember that it was also directed at large portions of his own work.

Cernuda's other book-length critical work is *Poetic Thought in English Lyricism.* This essay is a study of poetic theory rather than of poetry and limits itself to the nineteenth century, from Blake to Hopkins. Although a prefatory note points out that the book was dictated by circumstances rather than choice (circumstances having to do with his professional duties), it constitutes a tribute to a portion of a body of poetry which Cernuda considered unequaled and one of the glories of Western art (that is, English poetry). The study also offered him the opportunity of approaching in a formal way the thought of some of his favorite poets, such as Wordsworth and Browning. After historical overviews of the two main poetic periods involved, the romantic and Victorian, Cernuda proceeds to a straightforward exposition of each writer's theory. The chapters include biographical as well as poetic material and trace both the intellectual and poetic development of each poet in his historical background. Of special interest are the chapters on Wordsworth, with whose interpretation of nature Cernuda felt some affinities, and on Coleridge whose theoretical work he greatly admires. It is a work of cogent scholarship, clear and unpretentious, certainly of great usefulness to Spanish readers who have had little material available on the subject.

The rest of Cernuda's criticism, in the form of articles, attests to the poet's singularly broad literary interests. There are short pieces on Ronald Firbank and Dashiell Hammett, for instance, novelists who have only recently received critical attention,[13] as well as on such masters as Rilke, Yeats, and Eliot. Personal tributes are paid to Aleixandre, Altolaguirre, Lorca, and Gide. In Valle-Inclán, Cernuda finds the greatest Spanish dramatist of the present century, an opinion now more commonly held than it once was. His article on "Popular Poetry," which opens *Poesía y Literatura*, contains the first sketch of his theory on the relationship between spoken and written language in poetry: Manrique represents the highest expression of an equilibrium between these two strains, while with Garcilaso begins the movement toward purely "poetic" language. His own efforts tended, as we know, to a new fusion of both elements.

Apart from its intrinsic value, which is not small, Cernuda's criticism is indispensable reading for those who want to do a serious study of his work. One should know what he says about Wordsworth in order to understand better the shaping forces of his vision of nature, or about Browning, who revealed to him the power of dramatic lyricism. Likewise it is important to be aware of his preference for Garcilaso, Aldana, Manrique, and the anonymous author of the "Epístola moral." His critical work shows an incisive mind, thoroughly a poet's, for whom his art is the highest value. Perhaps in entitling his two volumes of essays *Poetry and Literature* he was thinking of the famous last line of Verlaine's "Art Poétique": "Et tout le reste est littérature" (What is not great poetry is mere "literature").

CHAPTER 9

Conclusion

CERNUDA was one of those few poets whose early and demanding poetic vision already accompanied an exceptional gift of words. The more specific aspects of that vision, however, were to define themselves more slowly than did his craft because of their profoundly existential character. Cernuda had to discover them within himself after arduous, wrenching efforts. They involved the acceptance of his homosexuality, a preference he did not fully realize until he was well into his twenties, and the rejection of traditional religious values with their customary ballast of social convention. And it is well to keep in mind these two positions as we read the poet's work, particularly from the surrealist period on, when they became firmly rooted. For Cernuda was totally engaged in the substance of his life and wanted to live it with passionate intensity.

Still, Cernuda knew himself to be a poet before he did a homosexual or a social inconoclast. In this sense it was language that first led the way for him and helped to clarify the issues. That is why, for instance, he devotes to it the first text of *Variaciones sobre tema mexicano (Variations on a Mexican Theme)* at an important juncture of his life when in his mind he had gone full circle and, as a poet whose exiled condition permeates his works, had found a second homeland: "The language that our people spoke before we were born of them, that which we use to know the world and take possession of things by means of its names, important as it is in the life of every human being, is even more so in the poet's. Because the language of the poet is not only the matter of his work but also the condition of his existence. . . .For poetry is the word."[1]

Poetry taught Cernuda to circumscribe the problematic areas of his existence—problematic with respect to society—and to turn them into instruments of a coherent perception of the world. The first part of this enterprise was accomplished after a period of turmoil, when

156

Invocations was published. By the time his next book of verse was completed, the Civil War was over and he resided in England. Concurrent with the second aspect of his work, the achieving of an encompassing outlook on reality, Cernuda's near mystical intuitions took form. The central part of his poetry, from *The Clouds* to *Living Without Being Alive* attends mainly to these concerns. In his last two collections of poems, *With Time Running Out* and *The Disconsolate Chimera*, the poet becomes more involved with circumstance: he had found a new home not unlike his native land in Mexico and known real erotic fulfillment. But whether plunged in the world's duration or trying to contain it, he gave himself wholly to the encounter.

Cernuda's lifelong contention with reality was born not of antagonism but of love. A passionate attachment to the momentary beauty of the tangible compelled his desire to fixate it, abstracting it from otherwise inevitable deterioration. Hence we find in a poet whose verse can reach spiritual summits unflagging attention to concreteness and an absolute implication of the self in the world's immediacy. But these extremes touch, as they have always in the great mystics and spirituals; indeed they must, for they are mutually dependent.

In the ethical journey marked out by his work, each of Cernuda's poems constitutes an attempt to redefine his existential relationship with the world and to seize it. For the world is his mirror also, and in capturing its passing aspects it is aspects of himself that he holds fast. This endeavor will increasingly admit of only the most essential, the barest descriptive tools, so that the rhetoric of enthusiasm is gradually replaced by the concision of cool evaluation. Fortunately, such spareness does not imply shortness of poetic breath; Cernuda continues to write until his death the long poem in which he always excelled and, near the end, gives us "Ludwig of Bavaria Listens to 'Lohengrin,'" one of his greatest.

His clarity, his total involvement, the broad spectrum of his concerns, all contribute to his importance as an early mentor of the present generation of Spanish poets. They acknowledge in him the first of the group of 1925 to express with impassioned logic the paradoxes of duration and to have made of ethical introspection the methodological cornerstone of his poetry. Poets yet to come will doubtless echo other facets of Cernuda's fertile verse whose imprint, if slow to emerge, remains indelible.

Notes and References

Chapter One

1. Luis Cernuda, "Generación del '25," in *Estudios sobre poesía española contemporánea* (Madrid, 1970), p. 146.

2. The classical lira was a strophe of five lines, the first, third and fourth of seven syllables, the second and fifth of eleven, with rhymes *a b a b a*. But there are also liras of four lines (*a b b a*) and of six (*a b a b a a*).

3. *Carmen*, no. 1 (December, 1927).

4. Quoted by C. B. Morris in *A Generation of Spanish Poets: 1920–1936* (Cambridge, 1969), p. 19.

5. Cernuda, *Estudios sobre poesía española contemporánea*, p. 144.

6. Ibid., p. 150.

7. Federico García Lorca, "Homenaje a Luis Cernuda," in *Obras completas* (Madrid, 1964), p. 158.

8. Cernuda changed the title of this first collection to *Primeras poesías (First Poems)*, when he incorporated it with the first edition of *Reality and Desire*. He also reworked most of the poems and excluded others. We must thank Mr. Derek Harris for having published an excellent critical edition with commentary and notes of this precious early book: Luis Cernuda, *Perfil del aire, (con otras obras olvidadas e inéditas, documentos y epistolario)*, ed. Derek Harris (London, 1971).

9. All English titles of Cernuda's individual collections are taken from *The Poetry of Luis Cernuda*, ed. Anthony Edkins and Derek Harris (New York, 1971).

10. All biographical data are taken from "Historial de un libro," ("History of a Book"), Cernuda's autobiographical essay, in *Poesía y literatura I y II* (Barcelona, 1971), pp. 177–215. Also useful were: Philip Silver, *"Et in Arcadia Ego": A Study of the Poetry of Luis Cernuda* (London, 1965); Derek Harris's edition of *Perfil del aire* (see note 8 above); Derek Harris, *Luis Cernuda, A Study of the Poetry* (London, 1973); the issue of *Insula*, no. 207 (1964), devoted to Cernuda, for details on his last years in Mexico and California; J. Capote Benot, *El período sevillano de Luis Cernuda* (Madrid, 1971) for information on Cernuda's early years.

11. Luis Cernuda, "Belleza oculta" ("Hidden Beauty"), in *Ocnos* (Xalapa, 1963), p. 48; hereafter cited in text as *0*.

12. Pedro Salinas, "Diez o nueve poetas," in *Ensayos de literatura hispánica* (Madrid, 1961), p. 354.

13. Luis Cernuda, "Historial de un libro," in *Poesía y literatura I y II* (Barcelona, 1971), p. 181; hereafter cited in text as *PL*.

14. See Luis Cernuda, "El crítico, el amigo y el poeta," in *Poesía y literatura I y II*, pp. 157–76; see also Harris, *Perfil del aire*, pp. 71–78, for detailed comments on the reception of *Perfil del aire* by the critics.

15. Harris and Edkins have not translated any material from this collection.

16. One of the Spanish Republic's educational projects through which artists and scholars brought some culture to remote parts of the country by means of lectures, performances of the classics, readings, and so on.

17. Luis Cernuda, "Palabras antes de una lectura," in *Poesía y literatura*, pp. 151–56.

18. Ibid., p. 152.

19. Ibid.

20. Ibid.

21. Ibid., p. 156.

22. Stéphane Mallarmé, "Un coup de dés," in *Œuvres complètes* (Paris, 1945), p. 477.

23. See *The Poetry of Luis Cernuda*, pp. 55–59.

24. "El poeta y los mitos," in *Ocnos*, p. 39.

Chapter Two

1. Luis Cernuda, "La luz," in *Ocnos*, p. 161.

2. We recall here Baudelaire's idea of the poet receptive to symbolic reality, particularly in the well-known sonnet "Correspondances."

3. We return to this matter in Chapter 4.

4. Reminiscent of the Gnostic "Logos." Among the sayings of Christ as the "Logos" in the Gospel of St. John is, of course, "I am the light of the world."

5. See Harris, *Luis Cernuda: A Study of the Poetry;* see also Silver, *"Et in Arcadia Ego": A Study of the Poetry of Luis Cernuda*.

6. See below.

7. See Chapter 1. Cernuda never spared his own work from criticism; in fact, he was often unduly severe.

8. Edkins and Harris, *The Poetry of Luis Cernuda*, p. 9; hereafter cited in text as *PC*.

9. Luis Cernuda, *La realidad y el deseo*, (Mexico City, 1964), p. 18; hereafter cited in text as *RD*. Translations except where noted are my own.

10. Contrary to Harris' suggestion in *Luis Cernuda: A Study of the Poetry*, p. 31.

11. See José Olivio Jiménez, "Emoción y trascendencia del tiempo en la poesía de Luis Cernuda," in *Cinco poetas del tiempo* (Madrid, 1964).

12. André Breton, "Second Manifeste du surréalisme," in *Manifestes du surréalisme* (Paris, 1970), pp. 76–66.

13. C. B. Morris, *Surrealism and Spain, 1920–1936*, pp. 57–58.

14. Ferdinand Alquié, *Philosophie du surréalisme* (Paris, 1955), p. 105.

15. The title of this poem is reminiscent of two lines in Baudelaire's "Spleen (Quand le ciel bas et lourd . . .)": "Et qu'un peuple muet d'infâmes araigneés/Vient tendre ses filets au fond de nos cerveaux. . . ."

16. Quoted in C. B. Morris, *Surrealism and Spain*, p. 80.

17. Baudelaire, *Selected Verse*, trans. Francis Scarfe (Baltimore, 1961), p. 190.

18. Gustavo Adolfo Bécquer, *Obras* (Barcelona, 1962), pp. 324–25.

19. See Harris, *Luis Cernuda: A Study of the Poetry*, p. 56.

20. For instance, in the plurals of *dichas* and *penas* translated as singulars "sorrow" and "joy" by Edkins: "Donde *penas* y *dichas* no sean más que nombres."

21. See Silver, *"Et in Arcadia Ego": A Study of the Poetry of Luis Cernuda*.

22. Luis Cernuda, "Palabras antes de una lectura," in *Poesía y literatura I y II*, p. 155.

23. John M. Robinson, *An Introduction to Early Greek Philosophy* (Boston, 1968), p. 96.

24. From "El viento de septiembre entre los chopos" (The September wind in the elms) *RD*, pp. 108–110.

25. "El poeta y los mitos" ("The Poet and Myths"), in *Ocnos*, p. 35.

26. Ibid., p. 36.

Chapter Three

1. See "The Consonance," in *Ocnos*, p. 191.

2. See Erich Neumann, *The Great Mother* (New York, 1955).

3. Derek Harris, *Luis Cernuda: A Study of the Poetry*, p. 74.

4. The title of this section is borrowed from Rupert Brooke's poem "Safety" in which the twelfth line reads: "Secretly armed against all death's endeavour."

5. See *The Poetry of Luis Cernuda*, p. 65.

6. Alexander Coleman, *Other Voices: A Study of the Late Poetry of Luis Cernuda* (Chapel Hill, 1969), p. 74.

7. I have transposed "also" in this last line.

8. Coleman notes the poem's resemblance to Yeats's *The Resurrection*. There are many acute observations in his study of this piece (pp. 96–106), particularly on the function of dramatization.

9. See Wordsworths's "Prelude."

10. The poem calls to mind the last lines of Baudelaire's "Un Voyage à Cythère": "—Ah! Seigneur! donnez-moi la force et le courage/De contempler mon coeur et mon corps sans dégoût!"

11. See Neumann, *The Great Mother*. This aspect of the earth mother would be the undifferentiated unconscious.

12. I borrow this phrase from Gerald Manley Hopkins' poem "Pied Beauty": "He father's-forth whose beauty is past change."

13. The other two are "Silla del rey" ("Seat of the King") in *Living Without Being Alive* and "Aguila y rosa" ("Eagle and Rose") in *With Time Running Out*.

Chapter Four

1. This statement is attributed to Heraclitus.
2. "La poesía" ("Poetry"), in *Ocnos*, pp. 9–10.
3. Ibid., p. 10.
4. Louis Massignon, *La Passion d'Al-Hallaj* (Paris, 1914–1921), p. 465.
5. Ibid, p. 467.
6. Ibid., p. 408.
7. Ibid., p. 468.
8. See Harris, p. 110.
9. See Silver, p. 178.
10. "Words Before a Reading," in *Poesía y literatura* p. 156.
11. See Silver, pp. 41–42.
12. "Mañanas de verano," in *Ocnos*, p. 41.
13. See Coleman, pp. 76–81.
14. "The Heath," in *Ocnos*, p. 142.
15. See Coleman, p. 85.
16. José Olivio Jiménez, *Cinco poetas del tiempo*, p. 120.
17. The *Tú* voice as a form of self-address is more striking in Spanish than it is in English, where the use of the impersonal "you" makes it less arresting.
18. "Tres poetas metafísicos," in *Poesía y literatura*, p. 51.
19. Ibid., p. 51.
20. Neumann, *The Great Mother*, p. 203.
21. See Chapter 2.
22. "El mirlo," in *Ocnos*, p. 140.
23. Ibid, p. 191.
24. Harris (p. 79) points out the echo of Quevedo in these lines.
25. There are several versions of a mystical recital which are reminiscent of this poem (For example, in Avicenna and Ahmad Ghazzali); the closest is in Attar's mystical epic, the *Language of the Birds*, where we read: "At that moment, in the reflection of their countenance, the Si-murgh [thirty birds] saw the face of the eternal Simurgh. They looked: it was veritably that Simurgh, without any doubt, *that* Simurgh was veritably *these* Si-murgh." See Henri Corbin, *Avicenna* (New York, 1955), p. 201. Borges' short story, "El Simurg," is the latest form of the same theme.

Chapter Five

1. Twenty-one out of thirty-one poems if we consider individually "Four Poems for a Shadow."
2. As we have seen, such importance given to sight is in the mainstream of mystical, Gnostic tradition, joining in love the human and the divine. See Plato, *Timaeus*, 47a–c.

3. See Chapter 3, pp, 58.
4. Silver, p. 126, n.26.
5. Plato, *Cratylus*, 402a.
6. Robinson, *An Introduction to Early Greek Philosophy*, p. 91.
7. Once again (see page 99 of this text) desire is linked to the power of vision.
8. According to Silver, the tree in question is probably a sycamore that Cernuda could see daily in the Fellows Garden at Emmanuel College, Cambridge.

Chapter Six

1. Cf. the Hapsburg Eagle.
2. The excellent study of this poem by Gonzalo Sobejano reached me when the body of my text was completed. I was happy to note that the thrust of his detailed analysis was similar to that of my own less elaborate exposition. I refer the reader to Gonzalo Sobejano, "Alcances de la descripción estilística (Luis Cernuda: 'Nocturno yanqui')," in *The Analysis of Hispanic Texts: Current Trends in Methodology* (Bilingual Press, 1976), pp. 89–112.
3. J. Olivio Jiménez, *Cinco poetas del tiempo*, p. 121.
4. The portrait hangs in the Boston Museum of Fine Arts where Cernuda saw it frequently.
5. There is here a reminiscence of Garcilaso's Sonnet V, in particular, the lines "por vos nací, por vos tengo la vida, / por vos he de morir y por vos muero." See Emilia de Zuleta, *Cinco poetas españoles* (Madrid, 1971), p. 450.

Chapter Seven

1. The title of this collection is taken from T. S. Eliot's "Burnt Norton" in *Four Quartets:* "The loud laments of the disconsolate chimera"; See C. P. Otero, "Cernuda en California,"*Insula*, no. 207, (February, 1964). pp. 1, 14.
2. Ibid.
3. Harris, p. 165.
4. The questions on the reaction of the beloved acquire even sharper relief in the case of homosexual love and the social stigma attached to it.
5. In the "Lohengrin" legend the young knight came on a boat towed down the Rhine by two swans and disappeared the same way.
6. The associations of this poem are reminiscent of Mallarmé's "Le vierge, le vivace et le bel aujourd'hui."
7. Such was the shout hurled at Unamuno by General Millán Astray, one of the leaders of Franco's rebellion.
8. See Octavio Paz, "La palabra edificante (Luis Cernuda)," in *Cuadrivio* (Mexico, 1965), p. 199.
9. See Chapter 1.

Chapter Eight

1. "Entrevista con un poeta," in *Poesía y Literatura*, p. 375.
2. In a note to the 1960 edition of *Poesía y Literatura I y II* Cernuda expresses the intention to forget all other articles not included in that volume.
3. See "Words before a reading" and "History of a Book," both in *Poesía y Literatura I y II*.
4. *Poesía y Literatura,* p. 378.
5. Ibid., p. 375.
6. "Cervantes (1941)," in *Poesía y Literatura*, p. 221.
7. *Estudios sobre poesía española contemporánea* (Madrid, 1957), p. 30; hereafter cited as *E*.
8. Ibid., p. 37.
9. Garcilaso was also a great favorite of Cernuda's, who preferred him (as he did San Juan de la Cruz) to Góngora. In this, as in other matters, he differed from other members of the Generation of 1925.
10. Apart from Mallarmé, these were not strictly symbolist poets.
11. Our introductory chapter dealt in some detail with Cernuda's view of the 1925 generation, and we refer the reader to that section.
12. See *Poesía y Literatura I y II*.
13. The work of Dashiell Hammett had been studied by Mme. Claude Edmonde Magny in *L'Age du roman américain* (Paris, 1948).

Chapter Nine

1. *Variaciones sobre tema mexicano* (Mexico City, 1952).

Selected Bibliography

PRIMARY SOURCES

Perfil del aire. 4th supplement to "Litoral." Málaga: Imprenta Sur, 1927.
La invitación a la poesía. Madrid: Ediciones "La tentativa poética," 1933.
Donde habite el olvido. Madrid: Editorial Signo, 1934.
El joven marino. Madrid: Colección "Héroe," 1936.
La realidad y el deseo. Madrid: Cruz y Raya, 1936.
Ocnos. London: The Dolphin Press, 1942.
Las nubes. Buenos Aires: Colección "Rama de oro," 1943.
Come quien espera el alba. Buenos Aires: Editorial Losada, 1947.
Tres narraciones. Buenos Aires: Editorial Imán, 1948.
Ocnos. 2nd ed., rev. Madrid: Colección Insula, 1949.
Variaciones sobre tema mexicano. Mexico City: Colección "México y lo mexicano," Porrúa y Obregón, 1952.
Poemas para un cuerpo. Málaga: Colección "A quien conmigo va," Imprenta Dardo, 1957.
Estudios sobre poesía española contemporánea. Madrid: Ediciones Guadarrama, 1957.
La realidad y el deseo. 3rd ed., rev. México City: Colección "Tezontle," Fondo de cultura económica, 1958.
Pensamiento poético en la lírica inglesa (siglo XIX). México City: Imprenta Universitaria, 1958.
Poesía y literatura. Barcelona: Seix Barral, 1960.
Desolación de la quimera. Mexico City: Joaquín Mortiz, 1962.
Ocnos. 3rd ed. Xalapa: Universidad Veracruzana, 1964.
La realidad y el deseo. 4th ed. Mexico City: Colección "Tezontle," Fondo de cultura económica, 1964.
Crítica, ensayos y evocaciones. Barcelona: Seix Barral, 1970.
Poesía y literatura I y II. Barcelona: Seix Barral, 1971.
Antología poética. Edited by R. Santos Torroella. Barcelona: Seix Barral, 1971.
The Poetry of Luis Cernuda. Edited by Derek Harris and Anthony Edkins. New York: New York University Press, 1971.
Perfil del aire. Con otras obras olvidadas e inéditas, documentos y epistolario. Edited by Derek Harris. London: Támesis Books Ltd., 1971.

165

166 LUIS CERNUDA

SECONDAY SOURCES

ADELL, ALBERTO. "El panteísmo esencial de Luis Cernuda." *Insula,* no. 27 (September, 1972) pp. 3,6. On Cernuda's moral philosophy.

AGUIRRE, J. M. "La poesía primera de Luis Cernuda." *Hispanic Review* 34 (1966), pp. 121–134. Emphasizes Cernuda's early artistic mastery in contrast with his imprecise emotions.

ALQUIE, FERDINAND. *Philosophie du surréalisme.* Paris: Flammarion, 1955. Useful theoretical background.

ARANA, MARIA DOLORES. "Sobre Luis Cernuda." *Papeles de Son Armadans,* no. 117 (1965), pp. 311–328. Focusses on Cernuda from a Heideggerian position.

BÉCQUER, G. A. *Obras.* Barcelona Editorial Vergara, 1962. Some models for Cernuda.

BRETÓN, ANDRE. *Manifestes du surréalisme.* Paris: Gallimard, 1970. Further relevant theory.

BRINES, FRANCISCO. "Ante unas poesías completas." *La caña gris,* nos. 6–8 (1962) pp. 117–153. [This entire issue of *La caña gris* is devoted to Cernuda] A poet's understanding of Cernuda. Stresses, in a review of all his work, Cernuda's total involvement with reality.

CANO, J. L. *De Machado a Bousoño. Notas sobre poesía española contemporánea.* Madrid: Insula, 1955 pp. 121–163. Cernuda as poet of evasion.

CAPOTE BENOT, J. M. *El período sevillano de Luis Cernuda.* Madrid: Gredos, 1971. For biographical data.

CIRRE, J. F. *Forma y espíritu de una lírica española (1920–1935).* Mexico City, Panamericana 1950, pp. 124–134. Cernuda as poet of love.

COLEMAN, ALEXANDER. *Other Voices: A Study of the Late Poetry of Luis Cernuda.* Chapel Hill: University of North Carolina Press, 1969. Excellent study of Cernuda's dramatic techniques.

DEBICKI, A. P. "Luis Cernuda: La naturaleza y la poesía en su obra lírica." In *Estudios sobre poesía española contemporánea.* Madrid: Gredos, 1968 pp. 285–306. How Cernuda avoids the dangers of subjectivism and generality by a judicious use of natural elements and the precision of his imagery.

DELGADO, A. "Cernuda y los estudios literarios.." *Cuadernos Hispanoamericanos,* no. 74 (1968), pp. 87–115. Overview of Cernuda's critical work, especially on poetry.

FERRATE, JUAN. "Luis Cernuda y el poder de las palabras." In *La operación de leer.* Barcelona: Seix Barral, 1962, pp. 209–232. Illuminating thoughts on Cernuda's surrealist period through stylistic analysis; also considers "Cementerio en la ciudad."

GIL DE BIEDMA, J. "El ejemplo de Luis Cernuda." *La caña gris,* nos. 6–8, pp. 112–116 (1962). Cernuda's present importance for the new Spanish poets.

HARRIS, DEREK. *Luis Cernuda: A Study of the Poetry.* London: Támesis

Books Ltd., 1973. Most complete and generally best work on Cernuda to date.

MORRIS, C. B. *A Generation of Spanish Poets: 1920–1936.* Cambridge: Cambridge University Press, 1969. General survey of Cernuda's generation, among best orientation in English.

———. *Surrealism and Spain.* Cambridge: Cambridge University Press, 1972. Contains valuable historical material.

MUNOZ, JACOBO. "Poesía y pensamiento poético en Luis Cernuda." *La caña gris,* nos. 6–8, pp. 20–25 (1962). Platonism in Cernuda's poetry.

OLIVIO JIMENEZ. J. "Emoción y trascendencia del tiempo en la poesía de Luis Cernuda." In *Cinco poetas del tiempo.* Madrid: Gredos, 1964 pp. 101–154. Very strong study of time in Cernuda. Stresses Cernuda's idealism.

OTERO, C. P. "Cernuda en California." *Insula* 207, no. 19 (1964), pp. 1, 14. Valuable information of Cernuda's final years.

PAZ, OCTAVIO. "La palabra edificante." *Cuadrivio.* Mexico: Joaquin Mortiz, 1965 pp. 167–203. Cernuda as ethical poet. Importance of his homosexuality. Excellent.

RUIZ, MARIO E. "La angustia como origen de 'La realidad' y manifestación 'del deseo' en Luis Cernuda." *Revista de Estudios Hispánicos* 5 (1971), pp. 343–362. Examines some philosophical aspects of Cernuda's work, but emphasizes to an extreme the poet's sensitivity to criticism and his fear of the unexpected and the irrational.

SALINAS, P. "Diez o nueve poetas." *Ensayos de literatura hispánica.* Madrid: Gredos, 1958. pp. 372–73. Early perceptive appreciation of Cernuda to *Invocations.* Finds Classicism first and later greatest distillation of romantic lyricism.

SILVER, P. "*Et in Arcadia Ego*": *A Study of the Poetry of Luis Cernuda.* London: Támesis Books Ltd., 1965. Stresses Cernuda's search for a lost Eden. Important and informative work.

SOBEJANO, GONZALO. "Alcances de la descripción estilística (Luis Cernuda: 'Nocturno yanqui')." In *The Analysis of Hispanic Texts: Current Trends in Methodology.* ed. Gary Keller. New York: Bilingual Press, 1976, pp. 89–112. Excellent, detailed study.

VALENTE, J. A. "Luis Cernuda y la poesía de la meditación." *La caña gris,* nos. 6–8 (1962), pp. 29–38. Examines technique of meditative poetry stressing the unifying power of Cernuda's mood and the total control it maintains over his works. Compares him to Unamuno as a passionate thinker.

ZULETA, EMILIA DE. "Luis Cernuda." In *Cinco poetas españoles.* Madrid: Gredos, 1971, pp. 396–418. General evaluation of Cernuda's poetry. Underlines meditative technique, Platonism; makes a distinction between love and desire.

Index